Austin's Old Three Hundred

The First Anglo Colony in Texas

By Their Descendants

Illustrations by Russell Autrey

EAKIN PRESS ★ Austin, Texas

Published in the United States of America
By Eakin Press
A Division of Sunbelt Media, Inc.
P.O. Box 90159 ★ Austin, TX 78709-0159
email: eakinpub@sig.net
website: www.eakinpress.com

2   3   4   5   6   7   8   9

ISBN 1-57168-291-0

Library of Congress Cataloging-in-Publication Data

Austin's old 300: the first Anglo colony in Texas.
    p.   cm.
Includes bibliographical references and index.
ISBN 1-57168-291-0 (hard)
    1. Texas—Genealogy. 2. Pioneers—Texas—Biography. 3. Texas—History—To
1846—Biography. I. Autrey, Russell. II. Title: Austin's old three hundred: the first
Anglo colony in Texas.
    F386.A95 1999
    976.4'009'9--dc21
    [B]   98-48360
                                                      CIP

For further information about Descendants of
Austin's Old Three Hundred,
contact:
Genealogy Department
George Memorial Library
1001 Golfview Drive
Richmond, Texas 77469

Land Commissioner de Bastrop and Empresario Austin
dispensing grant certificates

Contents

Foreword

On New Year's Day, 1830, Stephen F. Austin sat at his desk in San Felipe composing a petition to Commissioner General Juan Antonio Padilla on behalf of the early settlers of his first colony. As he set forth the arguments in favor of an augmentation of land for these first colonists, the reflections and reminiscences that often color the transition from the old to the new year may have pressed on Austin recollections of the time he was first informed of his father's bold project to settle three hundred families in the Texas wilderness and of the travails that subsequently attended the concretion of this enterprise. Foremost in his thoughts were the settlers who came with him in 1821 and 1822 and the steadfast fortitude they displayed in resisting the privations and dangers they confronted. The enterprising individuals, Austin wrote, laid the foundation of the colony in the heart of the wilderness, and the ensuing advances experienced in Texas were the result of their perseverance. Austin put it succinctly as he argued for his early colonists in the petition to Padilla: ". . . had it not been for the toils of the first [settlers] the others would have never come. In the beginning they risked everything, now there is no risk, no danger, no difficulty whatsoever."

In its inception the Texas venture was conceived by the Austins as a way to recoup the family fortune, and while Stephen may have eventually subsumed his initial desire for profit to what he came to perceive as his civilizing mission in Texas, most of the first colonists also came to Texas propelled by the hope of economic gain. The Anglo colonization of Texas was driven not by the search for greater political or religious freedom, the conscious advance of some preconceived manifest destiny, or by a utopian dream, but by the pursuit of individual economic self-interest. The glamorous episodes of history are often couched in terms of a struggle for some lofty cause, but the course of history has been changed as much by economic determinations as by the pursuit of these presumably loftier ends, and there can be no doubt that the successful rooting of the first Anglo colonists in Texas changed the history of this region. In retrospect, it was a decisive moment in the events that finally cost Mexico half of its national territory and completed the continental span of the American nation from the Atlantic to the Pacific Ocean.

The lure for these settlers was cheap land, and lots of it, and the distinction of being one of what came to be known as the "Old Three Hundred" emanated directly from being the recipient, through merit, design, or simple good fortune, of a land grant under the terms of Austin's first contract. Capricious fate deprived many other would-be settlers active in the inception of Austin's first colony of a land grant under the first contract and of the distinction this eventually conferred.

Austin's first contract was the only approved under the provisions of the 1823 Imperial Colonization Law of Mexico. Austin and a commissioner appointed by the governor were authorized to distribute the land to the settlers and issue titles to them in the name of the Mexican government. The quantity of land allotted to a head of a household was set at a minimum of one *labor* (177 acres) for farmers and one league (4,428 acres) for stock raisers, while those who professed both occupations could obtain a league and a *labor*. This amount could be increased without specified limits to settlers who had large families or to those who established new industries or were useful to the province or nation in other ways. The law stipulated that the land was to be cultivated within two years from the date of the title or run the risk of being forfeited, and several of the first contract grants were, in fact, voided for noncompliance with this provision. In the end, Commissioners Baron de Bastrop and Gaspar Flores issued 297 recognized titles between 1824 and 1828 under the first contract.

The process of distributing the land was not without its difficulties. Austin's desire to have a compact settlement was wracked by the "rambling disposition" of his settlers and the grants were scattered from the Lavaca to the San Jacinto rivers and from the coast to the San Antonio Road, with concentrations of grants in the most fertile areas. Although this complicated the task of protecting and governing the early colonists, Austin eventually recognized that the dispersion facilitated the settlement of later colonists over an extensive tract of land.

Land selections proved to be another source of difficulties. Every settler wanted a tract of land that was well-watered, fertile, and supplied with good timber and prairie, and disputes over land selections were inevitable and provoked dissension. Some of the settlers also complained about being slighted in the amount of land they were allocated by Austin, and others challenged his right to collect from them a fee of twelve and a half cents per acre for surveying the land and obtaining a title. As one might expect, civil disputes also arose among these independent and individualistic settlers, but in hindsight Austin suggested that the colonists had been freer of internal dissension than could be expected under the circumstances. To this assessment he added: "...they have borne with the most inflexible fortitude, all the privations, to which their situation exposed them, and have contributed largely, in laying a foundation for the future prosperity of Texas, by commencing the settlement of its wilderness." In many ways the first colony was the testing grounds of the Mexican colonization plan, and its success opened the way for further immigration and set the standard for later colonies.

Although scattered Anglo immigrants had been encroaching on the Texas frontier for years before the arrival of Austin's first settlers, these colonists were the first organized, approved influx of Anglo-American immigrants. Despite the undeniable hardships of the first years, several underlying conditions propitiated their survival and growth. The land was fertile and game was plentiful. The colony was set down in virgin country where there had been no Spanish or Mexican settlement, which precluded conflicts like those that later beset Haden Edwards. The colonists were allowed to govern themselves internally under the criminal and civil regulations set down by Austin and, above all, they had the invaluable guidance of a leader who oversaw the quality of settlers entering the colony, served as an intermediary with the Mexican authorities when friction arose over matters such as slave ownership and tariffs, and sought to further their general interests.

Austin's story is well-documented, but the story of his hardy colonists deserves to be expanded. Austin's first settlers constituted a diverse group of enterprising, persevering individuals, both men and women, and in the pages that follow the reader will be able to revive the adventures and contributions of these courageous colonists, through the accounts of the justifiably proud descendants of the pioneering constituents of the "seed colony of Texas," Austin's Old Three Hundred.

GALEN GREASER
Archives and Records Division
Texas General Land Office

Preface

Most of the information in this volume was first published by the Descendants of Austin's Old Three Hundred in 1991, under the title *The First Colony of Texas: Austin's Old Three Hundred*. The material in that book, now out of print, has been revised and other articles added for this publication.

The basic premise of the initial book has been retained: to provide glimpses of those who made up Stephen F. Austin's first colony as conveyed in the words of their direct descendants. The sketches reproduced here were either written or the information collected by one or more descendants of each subject.

Fewer than one-third of Austin's "Old Three Hundred" colonists are represented here. Some of the grantees were bachelors and received their land with one or more partners; others were either childless or their direct lineage has run its course. Still others are awaiting the time when their descendants will take up the challenge and provide us with something about their illustrious ancestor.

A word about the source materials for the biographies: There are six major sources that all, or nearly all, Old Three Hundred researchers utilize. Rather than repeat them in each bibliography, we cite them one time, as follows:

Barker, Eugene C., editor. *The Austin Papers.* 2 vols. Washington, D.C.: U.S. Government Printing Office, 1924-1928.

Bugbee, Lester G. "The Old Three Hundred," *Quarterly of the Texas State Historical Association,* vol. I, no. 2 (October 1897): 108-117.

Ray, Worth S. *Austin Colony Pioneers.* Austin: The Pemberton Press, 1970.

Tyler, Ron, editor. *The New Handbook of Texas.* 6 vols. Austin: The Texas State
Historical Association, 1996.
Webb, Walter P., editor. *The Handbook of Texas.* 3 vols. Austin: The Texas State
Historical Association, 1952.
White, Gifford. *1830 Citizens of Texas.* Austin: Eakin Press, 1983.

Please note that names reproduced in this volume are the original spellings as found in state and office records. For updated spellings where they occur, see the Ancestor Descendant lists in the Appendix.

Acknowledgments

The completion of the present volume could not have been accomplished without the assistance of many. Thanks to all who helped.

Past Presidents General Tim Cumings and Harry Howell gathered new biographies and corrections to the existing histories during their administrations.

Treasurer General Cheryl Kipp and I began compiling a corrected list of the men and women who came to this new land and received the original land grants from Mexico to make up the group of colonists now called "The Old Three Hundred."

Registrar General Wincie Campbell has researched the Lester G. Bugbee list of names and various spellings of each grantee's name at the Texas General Land Office. With the assistance of Third Vice President Shirley Stedman, she has established a list of land grant recipients our organization has adopted for use in determining future membership.

The Ancestor Book Committee, consisting of Mrs. Campbell, Mr. Howell, Mr. Cumings, and me, would like to express our sincere gratitude to W. M. Von-Maszewski, manager of the George Memorial Library's Genealogy/Local History Department at Richmond. His knowledge, skill, and the tedious task of helping the committee edit and then prepare a final draft is appreciated by our entire organization.

Mr. Galen Greaser, Spanish translator, Archives and Records Division of the Texas General Land Office, once again has written a Foreword for our second book. He writes of the importance of Austin's first contract and the beginning of the first major Anglo-American colony in Texas known as "The Old Three Hundred," the "seed colony of Texas."

Special acknowledgments go to the Descendants who submitted biographies of their ancestors to form the basis of this book. This publication would not have been possible without their commitment to this project.

DONNA M. (MRS. HUBERT E.) JOHNSON
President General 1996-1998

Biographies

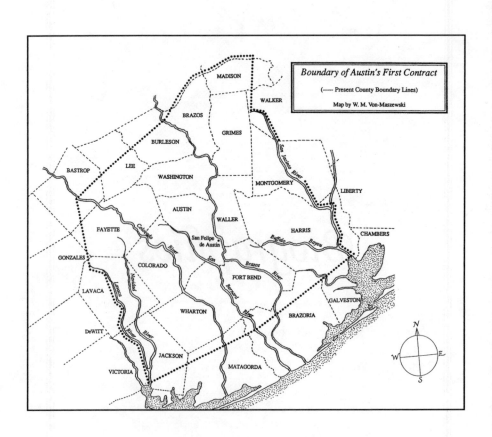

Boundary of Austin's First Contract

(----- Present County Boundary Lines)

Map by W. M. Von-Maszewski

MARTIN ALLEN

M artin Allen was born November 28, 1780, in Kentucky. He married Elizabeth Vice on September 27, 1804. She was born in Virginia. They had ten children.

In 1812 Martin joined the Gutierrez-Magee Expedition. His father, Benjamin Allen, was killed at the Battle of Medina in 1813. Martin moved to Arkansas Territory in 1817, then to Allen's Settlement, Louisiana, named in his honor. He then joined Stephen F. Austin's first colony, "The Old Three Hundred." In Texas in 1821, he was one of the first settlers on the Colorado River. In 1822, while he was back in the U.S. taking care of his ailing wife, he sent his sons Miles N. and James Bud to plant a crop and claim his land. Martin was granted one *sitio* of land in present-day Wharton County and one *labor* of land in present-day Austin County in July 1824. He and his family were in Texas in 1826 and appear on the first Texas census.

Martin signed the Loyalty Resolution to Mexico in 1827, was made a road supervisor in 1830, and was granted the right to operate a ferry across the Buffalo Bayou near Harrisburg. He also signed the call to the Convention in 1832, was made *regidor* of *ayuntamiento* at San Felipe, captain in the Civil Militia, and elected justice of the peace and land commissioner. The Allen family operated a "public house" for many years. Martin served in the Texas War for Independence. He gave much in goods and service to help Texas win its freedom from Mexico.

Martin died at his home at Eight Mile Point in Austin County in 1837, leaving an estate of 8,600 acres, animals, wagons, and slaves. Elizabeth died in 1843. Both are buried in the Allen-Johnston Cemetery on Allen's Creek. A Texas State Historical Marker was dedicated in 1993 to his memory and to his accomplishments in early Texas history.

Source:
Mrs. H. G. (Katherine Allen) Harrison #2

CHARLES G. ALSBURY

One of the elder sons of Capt. Thomas Alsbury was an early settler of Austin's first colony. Charles Grandison (or Grundison) Alsbury was born in Kanawha County, Virginia. He was on the Brazos River in August 1822 when the schooner *Lively* landed. Charles received a half-league as a part of grant No. 177, located on the west bank of the San Bernard River near the Gulf (now a part of the National Wildlife Refuge). He shared the grant with his brothers Horace and Harvey.

Charles Alsbury was politically active in the April 1824 colony election as well as in the December 1824 San Felipe election. In an incident in 1825, he came to the aid of a party of cold, wet, and tired Texans who were pursuing a mule thief. Two Kuykendalls, two Gateses, Moses Shipman, and others took a rest stop at Aunt Betty Whitesides' house, when all she could offer was cold buttermilk. Charles Alsbury pulled coffee out of his saddlebag and Aunt Betty made hot coffee for all.

Charles unsuccessfully tried to establish a town he called Monticello on his parents' grant at the mouth of Cow Creek. His own land grant was in the eastern end of the Karankawa hunting grounds. In fact, he was killed in 1828 while fighting in the Indian campaigns. His brother Harvey disappeared and was also presumed killed by Indians.

Source:
Delbert W. Whitaker #374

★ ★ ★

The alcalde *was the chief officer of the local government. As a sign of his office the* alcalde *carried a silver-headed cane, and when he could not appear in person, he could be represented by sending his cane.*

★ ★ ★

DR. HORACE ARLINGTON ALSBURY

The grant No. 177, made on August 3, 1824, gave Horace and his brothers, Charles and Harvey, half a league apiece on the west bank of the San Bernard River. Their father, Thomas Alsbury, also received a grant from Stephen F. Austin.

As a colonist who could understand Spanish, Horace was used on occasion to interpret the language of his adopted country. In August 1835, he authored an open letter warning the people of Texas about Santa Anna's intent to wage war.

Horace married Juana Navarro. She was the niece of Vice-Governor Juan Veramendi, James Bowie's father-in-law. Juana was in the Alamo when it fell, Horace having left her there for safekeeping. Earlier, Horace had taken part in the Siege of Bexar in Captain York's company.

Horace and his younger brother, Young Perry, served in the Texas Army's spy cavalry company during the Battle of San Jacinto. Along with six other men, they reportedly chased Santa Anna and his staff and cornered them at the recently burned Vince's Bayou bridge (Young helped scout Deaf Smith with that deed as well). Santa Anna was captured the next day.

In 1842, invading Mexicans captured Horace at Bexar Plaza in San Antonio and imprisoned him at Perote. He was released two years later, and in 1846 he and some of his brothers volunteered for duty in the U.S.-Mexican War. Horace was killed near Saltillo in the bloody last battle of Buena Vista.

Source:
Delbert W. Whitaker #374

★ ★ ★

"G.T.T." was the message left behind in the United States when settlers had GONE TO TEXAS.

★ ★ ★

CAPT. THOMAS ALSBURY

Stephen F. Austin may have seen the potential value in having the Thomas Alsbury family, with its seven sons and three daughters, become part of his colony. He wrote to his mother and sister urging them to have his brother contact and assist the Alsbury family in making the move from Hopkinsville, Kentucky, to Texas.

Long before, Thomas Alsbury had been a company commander in a regiment of Kentucky Mounted Volunteers during the War of 1812. He married Leah Jane Catlett of a prominent Maryland family. Thomas, born in Virginia in 1773, fathered his own family in Kanawha County, Virginia, and Christian County, Kentucky. He helped found Hopkinsville, where he was a major property owner and ran a sawmill and tavern. He held various public posts.

Thomas settled on grant No. 42 on the west bank of the Brazos River. One of his leagues was in present-day Brazoria County and one in Fort Bend County. He died August 15, 1826. The gravesite is unknown.

Source:
Delbert W. Whitaker #374

William N. Henderson to Stephen F. Austin

Opeolusas, 1st November 1821

Sir,

From a New Orleans Paper I have perused with much satisfaction an extract of a Letter from you to a Gentleman in that city and am highly gratified to find that you intend to carry into execution the noble enterprise contemplated by your honoured Father.

(Eugene C. Barker, editor, *The Austin Papers*, Washington, D.C.: Government Printing Office, 1924, vol. 2, part 2, p. 423)

WILLIAM ANDREWS

William Andrews received his grant, signed by Stephen F. Austin and Baron de Bastrop, on July 15, 1824. His land lay on the east side of the Brazos River. He was warned of his obligations to live on and cultivate the land for two years.

Andrews married Susan Clark on August 20, 1805, in St. Landry Parish, Louisiana. Six of their children were born there: Richard, Mary Ann, Micah, Joseph Zabulon, William Alexander, and Elizabeth. At least three were born after they came to Texas: Susan, Pamelia, and Walter.

The 1826 Census of Austin's Colony listed him as a farmer/stockraiser, between the age of forty and fifty, wife between thirty and forty, five children under sixteen, and two slaves.

Originally, William was against the idea of independence from Mexico, but he changed his views after the events leading to the battles of Anahuac and Velasco, and the imprisonment of Stephen F. Austin by the Mexican government.

Austin's call to arms came on September 19, 1835, as General Cos was moving his army into Texas. Two of William's sons, Richard and Micah, answered the call from Bastrop County. Both were wounded, and Richard died the next day. Micah lived to fight in the Battle of San Jacinto. Richard is said to have been the first casualty of the Revolution.

William Andrews died before January 10, 1840, leaving a substantial estate. Half was to go to his wife and the other half to be divided equally among his children.

Source:
Jonette Henson Ballmer #188

JAMES BRITTON BAILEY

Norther Carolina was the birthplace of James Britton Bailey in 1779. He was a descendant of Kenneth Bailey, whose ancestor was Robert Bruce, once King of Scotland. Bailey sailed from New Orleans to Anahuac, Texas, with his second wife Nancy and six children. They settled on the Brazos River, then called the Brazos District, in 1821. Three years later Stephen F. Austin legalized Bailey's claim by making him one of the Old Three Hundred grantees.

Brit Bailey was a hardy rancher and farmer. He became a friend to the Indian and on many occasions was peacemaker for the settlers.

James Bailey, Brit's youngest son, drowned in a river as a child. Phelps Bailey, second son, was killed by unfriendly Indians. Smith Bailey, number three son, was killed in the Battle of the Alamo. Betsey, the oldest daughter, was captured by Indians but escaped unharmed in the darkness of the night. The

Brit Bailey was one of the more colorful characters of the Old Three Hundred. Since his death and burial in 1832 at Bailey's Prairie, there have been numerous reports of his ghost appearing. It is said that the first sighting was in human form to Ann Thomas, who with her husband bought Bailey's place a few years after his death. Beginning in the 1850s the ghost has taken the form of a ball of light that appears on foggy nights and floats over the land and moves away when pursued. There are many stories of people watching the light roam the prairie.

In 1956 a gas well blew out and the fumes caused nearby Highway 35 to be closed for a week. Folks from around there said Brit did not want a well that close to his grave.

If some foggy night you are driving down Highway 35 just west of Angleton, across Bailey's Prairie, slow down and look very carefully. You may see Bailey's Light.

youngest daughter, Mary "Pollie," married Joseph Henry Polley, another Old Three Hundred grantee.

Stephen F. Austin arranged a meeting of the settlers on the Brazos River, in Bailey's home. Here they took an oath of fidelity to the Constitution of 1824. At this meeting a group of militia was organized. At Austin's request, Bailey was appointed lieutenant. In 1829 Governor Jose Maria Viesca bestowed on Bailey a commission as captain. In 1832 Bailey took part in the Battle of Velasco. Bailey had also served in the War of 1812.

Britton Bailey was a straight-shooting pioneer who endured many hardships. In stature he was a large man, feared and respected by Indians and neighbors. In December 1832, according to his request, he was buried standing up, facing west, with his rifle at his side, in the family graveyard on Bailey's Prairie.

Source:
George Bert Everts #196

★ ★ ★

Noah Smithwick wrote, "As one old lady remarked, Texas was 'a heaven for men and dogs, but a hell for women and oxen.'"

★ ★ ★

WILLIAM BARRET (BARRETT)

William Barret came to Texas as a single man, aged twenty-six, from Pennsylvania. He and Abner Harris were granted land in Austin's first colony on June 4, 1827, in Fort Bend County. Family tradition says that Barrret was kin to James Beard, another Old Three Hundred colonist.

One of the few documented acts of Barret's life was his marriage to Elizabeth Wiant on the east bank of the Brazos River. The marriage contract reads:

> Be it known that we William Barret and Elizabeth Wiant of lawful age of Austin Colony and state of [Coahuila] and Texas wishing to unite ourselves in the bonds of matrimony and there being no Priest in the Colony to Celebrate the same, Therefore I William Barret do agree to take and do hereby take Elizabeth Wiant to be my legal and lawful wife and as such to cherish support and protect forsaking all others and keeping myself true and faithful unto her alone. And I Elizabeth Wiant do agree to take and do hereby take William Barret to be my legal and lawful husband and as such to love honor and obey him forsaking all others keeping myself true and faithful unto him alone, and we also mutually bind ourselves to each other in the sum of five thousand dollars to have our marriage Celebrated by the Priest of the Colony or some other Priest Authorized so to do as soon as an opportunity offer, all of which we do promise in the name of God and in the presence of Alex[ander] Hodge Commissario and the other witnesses Present in Testimony whereof we have hereunto set our hands on the River Brazos this Eighth Day of July in the year of our Lord 1829.

To this union were born a son, Thomas William, on April 8, 1831, and a daughter, Elizabeth, who married Reuben Weir in 1846. Barret served in the Texas military offensive against Mexico in late 1835 under Capt. W. H. Patton and Commander

Edward Burleson. In 1841 he purchased 4,028 acres in Brazoria County. In 1853 Weir was made administrator of Barret's estate.

Source:
Deurene Oates Morgan #62

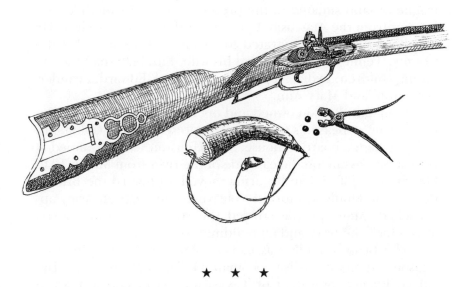

★ ★ ★

The first mention of a Texas Ranger force was by Austin in 1823. In 1835 the Provisional Government passed a resolution creating a corps of Rangers. There were three companies of twenty-five men to protect against Indians and bandits. They were paid $1.25 a day and had to furnish their own equipment. The reputation of the Texas Rangers was expressed by famous Ranger Col. John S. Ford, "The Texas Ranger can ride like a Mexican, trail like an Indian, and fight like the very devil."

★ ★ ★

Asa Mitchell settled at the mouth of the Brazos and had a salt works. He made salt by evaporating gulf water in large, shallow pans. Salt was used to preserve meat.

★ ★ ★

BENJAMIN BEASON

On August 7, 1824, Benjamin Beason received title to one league of land situated in the present county of Colorado, two leagues from the Atascosito Crossing of the Colorado River. He and his family had emigrated to Texas in 1822 from Hardin County, Tennessee. Beason and his wife, Elizabeth, had the following children: Lydia, Nepsey, Collins, Abel, Edward, Leander, Benjamin, and Mary Ann.

Benjamin Beason owned and operated a ferry on the Colorado River at Beason's Crossing, the present site of Columbus. His wife kept a boardinghouse. Sam Houston's army camped at Beason's Crossing on the east side of the river from March 19 to March 26, 1836. When his army moved on toward the Brazos, the Beason family was forced to leave as the Mexican Army approached. Many people crossed the river on Beason's ferry, after which the ferry and all buildings were burned.

The Beason family was in Harrisburg in April 1836. Mrs. Beason was an enterprising woman. On April 10 she wrote David G. Burnet, president of Texas, for permission to open a boardinghouse at Harrisburg for the support of the family until they could return home.

Beason died before March 9, 1837. His estate was probated in Colorado County in 1837 with Leander Beason and W. B. Dewees as administrators. Benjamin Beason's will is the oldest on record in Colorado County.

Source:
Nancy Jane Perry Wooten #242

ISAAC BEST

Isaac Best, the son of Stephen Best and, probably, Sarah Humphrey, was born about 1774 near Philadelphia, Pennsylvania. His wife was Mary Margaret Wilkins, the daughter of John Wilkins, born about 1776 in Kent County, Maryland.

They were married April 9, 1794, in Madison County, Kentucky. It was in Kentucky that Isaac and Margaret's first seven children were born: John about 1794; Isaac about 1796; Humphrey about 1797; Sarah "Sally," 1800; Phoebe, 1802; Mary "Polly," 1804; and Margaret "Peggy," 1807.

In 1808, Isaac moved his family to the Louisiana Territory. The couple had two more sons while living there: Ebenezer W. "Eben," 1808, and Stephen, 1810.

When Stephen F. Austin sought families to settle his new colony in Texas, Isaac, Margaret, sons Humphrey, Ebenezer and Stephen, and daughter Margaret, answered the call. They made the 800-mile journey by caravan, carrying not only their regular belongings, but their millstone as well. They arrived at the Brazos River on December 31, 1821. It was not until August 19, 1824, that they received a grant for one *sitio* of land on the east bank of the Brazos between the Cushatti (Coshate) and La Bahia roads. This was located near present Hempstead.

Isaac sold his original grant on October 8, 1828, to Jared E. Groce and bought a number of tracts on the east side of the Brazos near San Felipe. There he built his plantation.

Isaac died intestate on February 8, 1837. Margaret died intestate in February 1852.

A marker to the memory of Isaac Best and Mary Wilkins Best was placed by the Texas Historical Commission near Pattison in Waller County on September 1, 1974.

Source:
Eddie Wayne Bader #277

EDWARD R. BRADLEY

Edward R. Bradley was born in Fayette County, Kentucky, in 1760. His father, also Edward Bradley, came from Pennsylvania and was among those who crossed the mountains with Daniel Boone. Young Edward first married Molly Duncan; after her death, he married Elizabeth Winn around 1795. The twenty-year-old Elizabeth was kin to the prominent Lee family of Virginia. Her father George was wealthy and left land and slaves to all eleven of his children.

The Bradleys and their eight children came to Austin's Colony in 1822 to claim a grant. Oldest son Thomas and three sons-in-law—George Braxton Hall, David Talley, and Chester S. Gorbet—also received grants in the original colony. A daughter, Sarah Bradley Dodson, made the first lone-star flag of Texas in 1836 for her husband, Archeleus B. Dodson.

Edward's league of land was on the east side of the Brazos River, close to that of Talley and Gorbet. He was reportedly buried there in 1826. Elizabeth also buried five of her children before she died in 1843 and was buried alongside her husband.

Bradley has many descendants, but all spring from his five daughters and so none carries the Bradley name.

Source:
Jackie Thompson Waites #455

★ ★ ★

In 1827 there was a drought and the only rain that fell in the area was in present Wharton County on land that had been granted by Stephen F. Austin to John C. Clark. When other colonists heard about it, they would say that they were "going down to Egypt for corn," as matched the story in the Bible. That's how Egypt got its name.

★ ★ ★

CHARLES C. BREEN

Charles Breen's Mexican grant states that he came to Texas in 1825, to settle in Austin's Colony. The absence of Commissioner Bastrop prevented him from receiving a legal title to his land until May 24, 1827. His title was signed by the new commissioner, Gaspar Flores, and Stephen F. Austin.

Breen's property is recorded as league #40, on the west side of San Bernardo Creek, on the prairie called Bay Prairie. Today this land is in Brazoria County, not far from Sweeny. In fact, part is in the city limits.

The Breen family moved to Texas after their fourth child, Calton N., was born. It is believed that the Christopher Breen who lost his life in the Siege of Bexar was their son. Their two daughters were Mary and Hannah Elizabeth.

On the 1850 census they were listed in Williamson County, giving Charles' age as sixty-three and born in Georgia, and Martha as being born in South Carolina, and her age as fifty-five. Charles Breen died early in 1851.

According to the 1860 Williamson County census, Martha was living with her only surviving child, Hannah, and husband, John Knox Payne. Martha died February 12, 1890, and is buried in Lawrence Chapel Cemetery in Williamson County. To reach the cemetery, begin just south of Highway 95 overpass in Taylor, turning right on FM 112. Continue through Noack to Lawrence Chapel sign, 10.6 miles. From this sign to the cemetery is 2.9 miles.

Source:
Sherrill Louise Smith Johnson #336

15

WILLIAM B. BRIDGES

On July 17, 1824, William B. Bridges received a Stephen F. Austin grant of one league of land. This land was located on the Lavaca River, northeast of the present town of Edna, Jackson County.

Bridges' first wife died in Mississippi. Cynthia Ross and William Bridges were married in Mississippi in 1824. His first child by his second wife was born in Victoria County, on December 18, 1825. They had three girls—Mary, Martha, and Elizabeth. Cynthia died in Jackson County. The 1850 Census listed Bridges' birthplace as North Carolina, and his age as fifty-five.

The War for Texas Independence found Bridges serving in John Alley's Company. His service lasted two terms: October 3, 1835, to an honorable discharge November 25,1835; then from July 3 to October 1836.

He was a resident of Gonzales County in May 1838, where he proved that he was entitled to a *labor* of land (177 acres) because he had drawn a colonial grant of one league (4,428 acres) under Mexican law, and now under the Republic of Texas, was entitled to another *labor*. He received a patent (deed) for it in Gonzales County, in 1841.

Bridges married Eliza Lyons Tribble. They had six children: Amanda, Harriet, William B. Jr., John, Sophronoa, and Carrie.

William Bridges was elected justice of the peace in 1840 and 1845. The family had moved to Black Jack Springs, Fayette County, where Bridges died in March 1853.

Source:
Violet Ranne McElhinney #342

DAVID BRIGHT

David Bright, the son of George Adam and Mary Bright, was born in Augusta County, Virginia, in 1770. David married Judith Dinsmore, who was born in England and came to Amherst County, Virginia, with her father, James Dinsmore. Their marriage on June 6, 1799, was one of the first recorded in Augusta County.

David and Judith Bright's known children were Sarah Ann, who married Eli Hunter, John McCrosky, and William D. Lacey; Elizabeth, who married Noel Roberts; George, who was unmarried; Mary, who married Gabriel Straw Snider and Patrick Reels; and Haney, who married Thomas Jamison.

Bright and his family came to Texas from Illinois by way of Arkansas in 1822, landing near the mouth of the Colorado River. On December 20, 1823, he voted in the *alcalde* election at San Felipe de Austin. He was one of the electors in the Colorado District in April 1824 when Baron de Bastrop was chosen the Texas delegate to the state convention of Coahuila and Texas.

In 1823 and 1824, David Bright was a blazer who cut the brush for the chainmen of surveyor Horatio Chriesman in the Oyster Creek area of Fort Bend County. Bright received one league of land in Fort Bend and one *labor* of land in Austin County on July 15, 1824. These "Old Three Hundred" grants are recorded in the General Land Office in Austin.

The census of 1826 classified Bright as a farmer and stockraiser, aged over fifty. His household included his wife, a son, and a daughter.

In April 1836 the Bright family and the Patrick Reels family were camped near Liberty during the Runaway Scrape.

David Bright died September 2, 1837, and the petition of William D. Lacey to administer the estate was filed in Matagorda County on September 14, 1837. Judith Dinsmore Bright died

17

August 15, 1838, in Matagorda County. The final settlement of their estate was filed on March 2, 1842.

Source:
Donna McCrosky Johnson #23

"Taking of the Land"
(Closing statement contained in each grant document.)

. . . We put the aforesaid *(name of colonist)* in possession of said tracts, taking him by the hand, leading him over them, telling him in a loud and understandable voice that by virtue of the commission and the authority vested in us, and in the name of the Government of the Mexican Nation, we put him in possession of said tracts, with all their uses, customs, rights, and appurtenances, for him, his heirs, and successor; and the aforementioned *(name of colonist),* as a token of finding himself in real and personal possession of said tracts without any opposition, shouted, pulled grass, threw stones, set stakes, and performed the other necessary ceremonies, being notified of his obligation to cultivate them within the two-year term prescribed by the law; and in evidence thereof, we the aforementioned Commissioner Baron de Bastrop and Empresario Estevan F. Austin, hereunto subscribe with attendant witnesses, lacking a notary in the terms of the law, which we certify.

In the Town of San Felipe de Austin, on the 16th day of August of the year 1824.

("William Stafford" file, Box 4, Folder 6,
Texas General Land Office, Austin, Texas)

CAPT. JESSE BURNAM

J esse Burnam was born in Madison County, Kentucky, on September 15, 1792. He moved to Bedford County, Tennessee, with his mother, and six brothers and sisters. When Jesse was eighteen, his mother died, leaving him no money. On her deathbed, she urged him to be "honest and industrious."

In his twentieth year, Jesse wrote, "I married an orphan girl, named Temperance Baker, I made rails for a jack-leg blacksmith and had him make me three knives and three forks and I put handles on them. My wife sold the stockings she was married in, made by her own hands, for a set of plates. I traded a small piece of land and then we were ready for house-keeping. We used gourds for cups." His family and nine other families headed for Texas, settling at Pecan Point on February 15, 1821. Later they moved to the Colorado River, near present La Grange, in Fayette County.

Jesse's wife Temperance died May 4, 1837, leaving him with a large family of small children. Their children were William, Mary, John, Hickerson, Minerva, Nancy (said to be the first child born in Austin's Colony), Amanda, James H., and Jesse Bennett.

Jesse married Nancy Cummins Ross, daughter of James Cummins, another Colonist and widow of James J. Ross. Their children were: Emily Maria, Henry, Sadie Ellen, Waddy Linsecum, Adelia Lee, and Alice.

Nancy died on February 3, 1863, and Jesse died on April 30, 1883. They are both buried on the Burnam Ranch in Burnet County.

Capt. Jesse Burnam fought in the war with Mexico. He had served as a delegate from Colorado County to the Convention of 1832, the Consultation of 1835, as representative in the second session of the First Congress of the Republic of Texas, and as a member of the Council of the Provisional Government of the Republic of Texas.

Source:
Julia Nail Moss #26

Jane Long is known as the "Mother of Texas" because she had the first Anglo child in Texas. Jane was the wife of Dr. James Long, who led several expeditions to free Texas from Spain. On one such trip Jane accompanied her husband into Texas. Dr. Long left her with companions on Bolivar Point, opposite Galveston Island, while he went to Goliad.

After months of waiting for her husband's return all left except for twenty-three-year-old Jane, six-year-old daughter Ann, and the twelve-year-old servant, Kian. Jane could not be persuaded to leave and spent the winter of 1821–22 at Bolivar existing on birds, fish, and oysters. It was a hard winter and Galveston Bay froze. Indians were near, and when they approached, Jane flew a red skirt (petticoat) as a flag and fired the cannon to frighten them away.

Jane Long became one of the Old Three Hundred, later ran a boardinghouse in Brazoria, and after she moved to Richmond operated a hotel there. In later years she became a wealthy and influential woman.

MICAJAH BYRD

Micajah Byrd was born in Frederick County, Virginia, about 1789. He married Hannah Bradbury, born about 1795. They were among the first arrivals of Austin's colonists at La Bahia–Brazos River Crossing in 1821.

In talks with my grandmother in the 1930s, the granddaughter of Micajah Byrd said that the Byrds came from Virginia, where they had slaves but none were brought into Texas. The patent to the 4,428-acre grant was issued on July 10, 1824. Her mother told her also that she would sit on S. F. Austin's lap during his visits to their home.

Alden Hatch, in his biography of the Byrds of Virginia (1969), states that Micajah Byrd went to Texas with Austin in 1821. In the Texas census of 1823 and 1826, Micajah and Hannah Byrd were enumerated as being farmers and stockraisers with one female child at about six years of age. S. F. Austin picked his settlers well, as was exemplified by the stalwart Byrd family who took an active part in community affairs. Micajah served as an election judge in 1826-27 to elect an *alcalde*. He was on a committee that registered a protest condemning the Fredonian Rebellion. He was referred to as Major Byrd in the local defense force.

Hannah Byrd was a good, compassionate soul in caring for neighbors. My great-grandmother related the plight of a Mrs. Whiteside to Captain Chriesman, which resulted in the alleviation of much suffering.

Micajah Byrd fathered four daughters, my great-grandmother Nancy Byrd being the youngest. He died in 1830 during a yellow fever epidemic. Living close to the river with mosquitoes, a carrier of the disease, probably caused his early death. Hannah Byrd later married James Gray of Washington County. She died in 1862.

Source:
John Steven Howard #75

SYLVANUS CASTLEMAN

Sylvanus Castleman married Betsy Lucas in Davidson County, Tennessee. They immigrated to Sainte Genevieve, Missouri, by March 1822. There he signed on with Stephen F. Austin as one of the Old Three Hundred colonists.

Sylvanus first settled in the vicinity of Columbus, on Cummins Creek. He later received title to two *sitios* of land in present-day Wharton County. He also received two *labors* in present Austin County, on July 7, 1824.

On March 4, 1823, a list of American settlers in the Colorado District was made by Stephen F. Austin. Sylvanus Castleman was listed as being forty-six years of age, a farmer with cattle and hogs. His family at that time consisted of Elizabeth (thirty-seven), Nancy (eighteen), Sarah (seventeen), Elizabeth (thirteen), Lavena (eleven), Benjamin (seven), and Jacob (two).

On December 3, 1823, Stephen F. Austin appointed Sylvanus judge for the election held in the Colony for *alcalde*. Castleman was elected by 12 of the 17 votes, and took office on January 26, 1824.

The exact date of death and the place of burial is unknown, but at the July term of court in 1841, in Fayette County, Sylvanus' estate was partitioned among his wife, children, and grandchildren.

It is known that in his latter days, he had moved to the west side of the Brazos, about ten to twelve miles above San Felipe. It was here that he became deranged and committed suicide.

Source:
Kathy Faul #132

JOHN CRIER

J ohn Crier was born in 1790, son of Morgan Cryer and Barbara Morris.

The Crier family moved to Camden County, Georgia, in 1786 and also lived in East Florida where John was baptized May 12, 1790, in St. Augustine Parish. They later moved to West Florida and then to the Arkansas Territory. John's first wife, Cynthia, died some time before he departed Arkansas for Texas. Cynthia was the mother of Andrew and Tolitha.

John Crier received title to one league of land on June 6, 1827, through Stephen F. Austin's first *empresario* contract with the Mexican government. The land is located in what is now Matagorda County.

John later took up land in Fayette County. He was one of the founders of Fayetteville, along with Judge James Cummins and Capt. James Ross. He and Jesse Burnam were the first to plant cotton in Fayette County in 1834.

About 1832 John married again. His second wife was Polly Duty, and they had at least five children.

In 1836 John moved to a home along the Colorado River in Colorado County.

It is reported that John Crier was killed by Indians in March 1856 and buried on the edge of Ross' Prairie, between Ellinger and Fayetteville.

Source:
Mary Elizabeth Thompson Haecker #229

REBEKAH CUMINGS

Rebekah Cumings (circa 1757-1832), one of Stephen F. Austin's Old Three Hundred colonists and mother of James, William and John Cumings, also Old Three Hundred colonists, received title to a league and two *labors* of land in present-day Brazoria and Waller counties on July 21, 1824. However, she made her home north of San Felipe in the vicinity of the sawmill and gristmill built by her sons on Palmetto (later Mill) Creek in present-day Austin County.

Rebekah Russel was born in Loudoun County, Virginia, to Samuel and Sarah (Moore) Russel. Prior to 1777, she married Anthony Cumings, a Loudoun County property owner.

Perhaps also prior to 1777, Anthony and Rebekah Cumings relocated on the Ohio River in what is today Lewis County, Kentucky. The family operated a water-powered sawmill and horse-drawn gristmill prior to 1800.

They had seven sons and two daughters, in this probable order of birth: Samuel, Thomas, Anthony, John, William, James, Rebecca, Sarah, Robert. Rebekah was widowed prior to 1807.

In 1822, Rebekah, her three unmarried sons James, William and John, and daughters Rebecca and Sarah, traveled to Texas and became part of Austin's original colony. Rebekah, who died in the early part of 1832, outlived all but John and Rebecca. William, who had married in Lewis County, Kentucky, in 1824 and died on Mill Creek in 1828, left the only surviving child of the Texas family members, Samuel Anthony Cumings.

The spelling of Rebekah Cumings' name is taken from the signature on her will, made out in 1825.

Source:
Timothy Austin Cumings #18

24

JAMES CUMMINS

James (Jack) Cummins was born in 1774, in North Carolina. He married Elinor Mariah Waller, January 13, 1799, in Davidson County, Tennessee. By June 1822, he was in Texas as one of Austin's Old Three Hundred and was located on the Colorado River. On August 16, 1823, at San Felipe de Austin, he was elected *alcalde* of the Colorado District, and served in this capacity for four years.

Cummins and a group of settlers helped to put down the Fredonian Rebellion at Nacogdoches.

On July 27, 1824, he was granted six leagues of land and one *labor* of land in Colorado and Austin counties after he agreed to build a sawmill and gristmill on Cummins Creek in Colorado County.

Evidently, his first wife, Elinor, died before he came to Texas, leaving him with three small daughters, Maria, Eliza, and Nancy. The March 4, 1823, census of the Colorado District lists him married to Rebecca with a five-year-old son. Rebecca Crier was the daughter of James Crier, another colonist. Besides the five-year-old Willie (or Wylie), James and Rebecca also had two daughters, Harriet and Sarah.

When James Cummins' second daughter, Eliza, married John H. Moore, a famous Indian fighter, on June 14, 1827, her bridal dress was described as "the only one worn by a daughter of the Old Three Hundred: it was of fine white muslin brought from the States and trimmed with ruffles and frills of the same." This was according to Julia Sinks.

Because he was forty-nine years of age, James did not take part in the Texas Revolution. He died in 1849. His burial place is unknown.

Source:
Julia Nail Moss #26

JAMES CURTIS, SR.

James Curtis, Sr., was given land on August 3, 1824, in Burleson County, Texas, on the west side of the Brazos River. He was a stockraiser. In 1831 he moved his family to Bastrop County. He lived with or near to his orphaned grandsons, James and John Stewart. The Stewart land was on the west side of the Colorado River south of Bastrop.

Curtis served in the Texian Army during the Texas Revolution. He participated in the Siege of Bexar. James, Sr., substituted for a son on February 22, 1836. He was under J. J. Tumlinson's command. When the Mexicans came to Bastrop, he went to San Jacinto with Major Williamson and into Jesse Billingsby's company during the battle. Battle officers' reports estimating Curtis' age are incorrect.

James Curtis, Sr., was born circa 1779 in Spotsylvania County, Virginia, to Frances Carter and Rice Curtis III. He married Sarah Hercules on May 13, 1802, in Davidson County. He was twenty-three years old at the time.

He moved his family to Warren County, Tennessee, in about 1811. Sometime after 1820, he moved his family to Alabama. The Curtis family was in Texas by late 1823. Sarah Hercules and James Curtis, Sr., had nine children.

James Curtis, Sr., died in 1836 in Bastrop County, according to a signed statement by M. Elizabeth Curtis Reid. No gravesite has been found for him or his wife, Sarah. It is presumed that he was buried in a family burial ground possibly on Stewart lands in Bastrop County.

Source:
Charles Reid #318

26

JAMES CURTIS, JR.

James Curtis, Jr., was born to Sarah Hercules Curtis and James Curtis, Sr., in Davidson County, Tennessee, near Whites Creek in about 1806. His family later moved to Warren County, Tennessee. The Curtises were stockraisers and farmers. The family later left Tennessee for Alabama.

James married Polly Ann Hide in Jefferson County, Alabama, on June 11, 1823. The couple accompanied James' parents to Texas. James was given land on the east side of the Brazos River in present-day Brazos County. He later moved to Bastrop County near Curtis family members.

Polly Ann and James were recorded on the 1829 S. F. Austin Census and were childless at the time. James married a second time to Tamer C. Gray, daughter of Daniel Gray, sometime before 1843. The couple had one child, Sarah Ann, born in 1843. Tamer and James divorced in 1848. James married a third time to a woman named Rebecca. The third marriage was a short one as he died of consumption the following year.

James shows Republic of Texas service under Burleson from July 27, 1837, to November 9, 1837. He served as a private in Jesse Billingsby's Company in the Texian army during the Woll Expedition in 1842. James is also mentioned by J. H. Jenkins as one of four men attacked by Comanches during a mustang hunt near Plum Creek in July of 1842.

Source:
Charles Reid #318

CHARLES DeMOSS

Charles DeMoss was a man of vision and a true pioneer. At least twice he moved his family into frontiers where they were among the first to domesticate the wilderness.

In 1795 Spain thought it advisable to populate Upper Louisiana Territory as a barrier to the English in Canada, and offered inducements to settlers. A settler could get about 640 acres of land for as little as $41, according to his position, size of his family, and ability to cultivate land.

Taking advantage of this, Charles and his wife Martha, and their son Peter, who was born in Ohio, went to Cape Girardeau, Missouri, in 1802. He cultivated this land, raising corn and flax and hemp. Over the years seven children were born: Sally, Lewis, John, William, Loraharney, Martha, and Elizabeth. They remained in Missouri until 1824, when Stephen F. Austin's colonizing in Mexico beckoned them to move on. Charles and Peter were in the first three hundred families. Son Lewis is listed in an Austin register as arriving as early as 1823, but was not granted land until later.

They landed in Matagorda County, and eventually, all lived on Caney Creek, farming and raising stock.

Unfortunately, Charles' time was short in Texas because he and Martha died in 1826. His sons remained, raised families, and helped in the struggle to make Texas a republic.

Source:
Hardy Sanders #138

JOHN FOSTER

John Foster, who was born May 25, 1757, moved to the Natchez District with his family from South Carolina before 1784. They settled along St. Catherine's Creek in Adams County and later he settled in Wilkinson County.

On October 26, 1797, he married Mary Smith, born October 10, 1772, the daughter of Zachariah and Frances (Prestwood) Smith of Anson County, North Carolina.

John Foster's children were as follows: Gideon, John, Sarah, Randolph, Isaac Guilford, Moses A., Elizabeth, Nancy (Ann) D., Barsheba Hetty, John Claiborne, Mary Elizabeth, Augustus Rodney, George Poindexter.

In 1822, John and two of his sons, Isaac and Randolph, came to Texas as part of Stephen F. Austin's "Old Three Hundred" settlers. On July 14, 1824, he was granted two and a half leagues and three *labors* of land because of his good qualities; his well-known application to agriculture, stockraising, and industry; and his very large family. This was approximately 12,000 acres, the largest original land grant in Fort Bend County.

In November 1826, John Foster was commissioned to buy a steel mill in New Orleans. William B. Travis acted as Foster's attorney in January 1834.

Three of John's sons, John Jr., Randolph, and John Claiborne Foster, helped Texas in its struggle for independence. Several of his grandchildren fought in the War Between the States.

Nearing the age of eighty years, John Foster returned for a visit to Wilkinson County, Mississippi, where he died at the home of Maj. Francis B. Mayes, his son-in-law, on January 26, 1837.

Source:
Nadine Foster Zvolanek #343

RANDOLPH FOSTER

Randolph Foster, son of John Foster, was born March 12, 1790, in Mississippi. He became friends with Randall Jones when they served together in the War of 1812. After the war he returned to Mississippi.

During the period of 1817-1819 he visited the Fort Bend area prospecting for a place to settle. New Year's Day of 1822 found Foster serving as hunter for Stephen F. Austin's camp. That same year, he and family members returned to Texas and applied for land in Austin's Colony. Randolph's grant was on the Brazos River and included his earlier camp.

In 1828 Randolph returned to Mississippi and in Woodville on February 22, 1829, he married Lucy Ruffin Hunter. She was the daughter of William and Lucy Ruffin Hunter. Randolph and his bride returned to Fort Bend and settled on the John Foster grant.

They were parents of the following children: Isaac Prestwood, Nancy Adaliza, Mary Louise (who married Sid Winston, Jane Long's descendant), Lucretia Collitanius, Caroline Amelia, Lucy Matilda, and Randolph Guilford.

Randolph Foster, known to his family and friends as "Uncle Ran," was no ordinary man. For years he would take his horse and gun, leaving his home to spend months camping in what is now Arkansas.

Foster died August 18, 1876, in the home of his daughter, Mrs. Mary L. Blakely, of Fort Bend County. His wife, Lucy, preceded him in death on March 25, 1872. It is reported that they are buried on the homestead in Fort Bend County. There is a marker in the cemetery at Fulshear, but it bears no evidence that he is buried there.

A painting of Foster with Stephen F. Austin and Deaf Smith hangs near the Speaker's stand in the House chamber at the Capitol in Austin.

Source:
Winnie Rhea Cowgill #47

The first year was a hard one for the colonists. There was a shortage of tools, insufficient seeds for planting, and little rain, so the first corn crop was a failure. Families did without bread. Martin Varner told a story about his little son's first experience with a biscuit. Mr. Varner had managed to buy or trade for a barrel of flour. "Mrs. Varner made a batch of biscuits, which considering the resources of the country, were doubtless heavy as lead and hard as wood. When they were done Mrs. Varner set them on the table," according to Noah Smithwick. The boy picked one up, looked at it, and headed for the door. In a few minutes he came back and got another. Mr. Varner followed him outside to see what he was doing. He punched holes through the center, inserted an axle, and triumphantly displayed a miniature Mexican cart.

★ ★ ★

CHURCHILL FULSHEAR, SR.

The 1800 Census of Craven County, North Carolina, lists Churchill Fulshear as single, but he entered into a marriage bond with Betsy Summers of Craven County in New Bern, North Carolina, December 9, 1800.

In the fall of 1823, the Fulshear family and a weatherbeaten band of homeseekers from Tennessee made their way into Texas to join Stephen F. Austin's seed colony in Coahuila y Tejas, Mexico. When they reached the lower Brazos River they made their way upstream to the cabin of William Morton where Richmond stands today.

Preserved in Fort Bend County is a faded Mexican land grant made out to Churchill Fulshear, the elder, and dated July 16, 1824.

The Census of March 1826 listed Fulshear as a farmer and stockraiser, aged over fifty, and his wife aged forty to fifty. Noah Smithwick was a visitor in the Fulshear home in 1827 and described the old seaman as homely and lame, but noted for his generosity. He was elected *regidor* in 1830 and as such served on a committee to check the merits of land grantees in the Austin Colony. His succession papers state that he died January 18, 1831. No mention is made of his wife, so it is presumed she died between the 1826 Census and his death in 1831. It lists his children as Churchill Fulshear, Jr., Mary L. Fulshear Scobey (married to Robert Scobey, another Old Three Hundred settler), Benjamin Fulshear, and Graves Fulshear.

Several sources state that he was a mariner and a man of considerable property. His succession papers include a detailed inventory of his land holdings, farm equipment, livestock, furnishings, twenty-nine books (including *The Holy Bible, Memoirs of General Jackson, Dilworth's Arithmetic, Acts of Congress 1812, Sequel to the English Reader*, S. F. Austin's pamphlet, *Christian Morals, Treatise for Raising Sheep, Dilworth Spelling Book*), notes due him, and his brand of *CF.*

Sources:
John Emmette Kipp #113
Mrs. Gerald Floyd Inman #371

Marriage Bond

Be it known by these present that we John Crownover and Nancy Castleman of lawful age inhabitants of Austin's colony in the Province of Texas wishing to unite ourselves in the bonds of Matrimony, each of our parents have given Their Consent to our Union, and there being no Catholic Priest in the Colony to perform the Ceremony—therefore I said John Crownover do agree to take the said Nancy Castleman for my legal and lawful wife and as such to cherish and support and protect her, forsaking all others and keeping myself true and faithful to her alone, and I the said Nancy Castleman do agree to take the said John Crownover for my legal and lawful husband and as such to love honor and obey him, forsaking all others and keeping myself true and faithful to him alone. And we do each of us bind and obligate ourselves to the other under the penalty of twenty thousand Dollars to have our Marriage solemnized by the Priest of this or some other Priest authorized to do so as soon as the opportunity offers, all of which we do promise in the name of God, and in the presence of Stephen F. Austin, Judge and Political Chief of this Colony and the other witnesses hereto signed— Witness our hands the 29th of April 1824.

Witnesses present

(Adapted from *Marriage By Bond In Colonial Texas,* by Bennett Smith, Fort Worth, Texas: The Author, 1972, p. 67)

WILLIAM GATES

William Gates was born circa 1760. In 1783 he was paid for service as a soldier in the Revolutionary War from the state of North Carolina. Records show he was already married to Catherine Hardin.

Soon after the war, Gates immigrated to Tennessee, where a daughter Sarah and a son Samuel were born, 1783 and 1789 respectively.

Gates left a trail of records as he traveled through Kentucky, where in 1790, as an inhabitant of Lincoln County, on the waters of the Cumberland River, he signed a petition to the General Assembly of Virginia, asking for a county to be laid off south of Green River to the Ohio River.

While in Kentucky, William and Catherine had more children: Hanna, Charles, Amos, Ransom, Jane, and William.

About the year of 1810, William Gates took his large family to the Cadron Settlement in Arkansas. From there he headed for Texas for free land, wild horses, and game. He reached Nacogdoches December 27, 1821, and continued the journey westward. He found all the rivers fordable and reached the Brazos early January 1822. There in the rich river bottom, near Washington-on-the-Brazos, Gates and his family made their home.

William Gates received his land grant in 1824 from the Mexican government. While visiting his son Charles in San Augustine County, Gates died on August 6, 1828.

Source:
Elizabeth L. Armstrong #118

34

CHESTER S. GORBET

Chester Spalding Gorbet was born in 1790. He was granted a league of land July 19, 1824, according to Brazoria County records. It was situated on the east side of the Brazos River near the Gulf of Mexico. A petition was issued in 1824 by thirty-three men of the lower Brazos, stating that they were in favor of slavery and the privilege of selecting their own officers, both civil and military, and in all cases to be tried by jury. The first signature on this document is Gorbet's.

The marital history of Gorbet is confusing. Among the Gorbet Papers is a certificate of marriage to Ann R. Bradley, dated September 2, 1831, signed by Father Muldoon. In the 1836 census of Austin's Colony, Chester S. Gorbet is listed with wife Nancy and son Edward. They actually had five children: Dulcenia, Elizabeth, Edward B., Juliana, and Susan B.

It has been recorded that Gorbet was in the Grass Fight, the Battle of Bexar. He was one of the three hundred who answered the call of Old Ben Milam. He had joined the Texas Revolutionary Army on October 3, 1835. He was discharged on February 20 or 28, 1836, missing the Battle of San Jacinto by only a couple of months. He served in the Regiment of the Rangers from June 1, 1836, to January 11, 1838.

On June 24, 1844, he married Nancy White Wilson, a widow with six children. This is recorded in Montgomery County.

Gorbet was one of seven Baptists in the first Old Three Hundred families, and a charter member of the Reliance Baptist Church in Anderson, Texas, 1847.

Chester and the second Nancy had two sons: John T. and Lorenzo W. Gorbet. Chester Gorbet died on October 23, 1878. His burial place is unknown.

Source:
Lawrence A. Maddox, Jr., for his son Frederick Andrew Maddox #276

COL. JARED ELLISON GROCE

Jared Ellison Groce II was born in Halifax County, Virginia, to Jared E. and Sarah (Shepherd) Groce on October 17, 1792. Before coming to Texas, Groce was active in business and politics in Georgia and Alabama. In Alabama he became a substantial planter and slaveholder.

Groce set out for Texas in the fall of 1821, with a hundred slaves as well as cattle, sheep, hogs, horses, and a caravan of fifty wagons. He was granted ten leagues of land by the Mexican government in 1824 "on account of the property he has brought with him." Three leagues were in present Brazoria County, five in Waller County, and two in Grimes County.

Groce located Bernardo Plantation on the east side of the Brazos River, below present-day Hempstead. His rambling home was crafted so that it did not resemble what it was—a log house. Rooms were twenty feet square, floored with ash and equipped with fireplaces. For many years it was the showplace of the colony.

Jared Groce was the wealthiest of the Old Three Hundred and lived in a splendid home. In 1827 his daughter Sarah Ann graduated from a finishing school in New York and was coming to Texas. As the servants prepared the house for her arrival, they bemoaned the fact that the china was cracked and broken from the trip to Texas. A houseguest, Mr. White, who was a silversmith, provided a solution to the problem. Mr. Groce had a large collection of Mexican silver dollars, which Mr. White converted to bowls, cups, and plates.

When Sarah married William H. Wharton, she asked her father if she could convert the rest of the silver dollars to knives, forks, and spoons. The silver, with instructions, was sent to a New York silversmith. These silver pieces have been handed down through the generations.

The first Texas cotton was raised there and the first bale ginned in 1826. Groce has been called the "Father of Agriculture" in Texas. In 1831 he divided his holdings among his sons and built another home, called Retreat. Early in 1836 the fleeing provisional government of Texas found refuge for a while at Retreat, and from Groce's fields Sam Houston's army was fed—even though Groce in 1833 had opposed separation from Mexico.

Groce died of malaria on November 20, 1836. His grave is in the Hempstead Cemetery, marked by a section of the Bernardo Plantation entry gates.

Source:
Mrs. John Emmette Kipp #3

★   ★   ★

In Texas in 1823 dress material or any kind of cloth sold for seven to ten dollars a yard, a cake of soap was a dollar and a quarter, buttons were a dollar a dozen, men's socks were a dollar and a quarter a pair, and silk handkerchiefs were two dollars each. Few Texians could afford these things.

★   ★   ★

Though 1821 and 1822 were years of hardship and hunger for some, there was a spirit of kindness and sharing among the colonists. Horatio Chriesman, later Austin's surveyor, heard that a woman and her two sons were surviving on lettuce and little else and her husband was away in the United States on business. Chriesman was staying with Martin Varner, who was a very good hunter. When he told Varner of the situation, the hunter picked up his rifle and went into the woods. He soon was back with a large buck. Chriesman threw the buck on the back of his horse and immediately took it twenty miles to the family.

★   ★   ★

SAMUEL C. HADDY
(HADY, HEADY)

The origins of the Haddy family and how they arrived in Texas are not known. Samuel's wife was Elizabeth Chatham. They had four children: Eunice, Arnold William, Sarah Haddy Kelly, and Susan Haddy Callihan.

Haddy is listed as a stockraiser and farmer in various censuses. He died in February of 1831. He received a Spanish land grant of one *sitio* on August 19, 1824. This grant was located six miles east of San Felipe in what is now Waller County near the town of Pattison.

In 1842 the Austin County Probate Court appointed William Kelly administrator of Haddy's estate.

Source:
Carolyn Marble #364

★ ★ ★

The Old Three Hundred were a social people. They had dances with a fiddle usually providing music. On the Fourth of July they had barbecues. The children would play under the trees, young people would dance, and the men would talk politics. Weddings were special occasions to celebrate. After the ceremony there would be a wedding supper followed by a lively dance.

★ ★ ★

38

ALEXANDER HODGE

The Hodge family was camped in a grove of trees near Lynch's Ferry when the Battle of San Jacinto erupted. Alexander Hodge stood silent near a pine tree. At last, a rider passed their camp and called to them that the war was over, the Mexicans defeated. They all fell to their knees, crying, and prayed their thanks to God—even the grandfather. These are the memories recorded by his granddaughter, Clarenda Pevehouse Kegans.

Judge Hodge returned to Hodge's Bend on Oyster Creek, but the exposure and strain of the journey took its toll. He died August 17, 1836, and is buried in the family cemetery beside his wife, Ruth, who died in 1831.

Hodge's Bend Cemetery, one of the oldest in Fort Bend County, has been marked by the Daughters of the American Revolution as well as the Texas Historical Commission.

Hodge was born 1760 in Cumberland County, Pennsylvania, the son of William Hodge, grandson of John Hodge, residents of West Pennsborough Township. There is evidence that his mother was Mary Elliott, daughter of James Elliott, also of Cumberland County.

Alexander migrated as a youth to Edgefield District, South Carolina, and served under Gen. Francis Marion during the American Revolution. He married Ruth, then moved to Oglethorpe County, Georgia, where his children were born. They were: Archibald born 1790 married Charlotte Reeves; William born 1792 married Margaret Welch; Ruth born 1793, married William Harris; Nancy born 1794; John born 1796 married Elsie Smith; Alexander Elliott born 1800 married Elizabeth Barnhill; Mary born 1801 married James Pevehouse; James born 1803 married Zulema Kuykendall; Cynthia born 1805; and Lucinda born 1809 married Stephen Richardson.

Hodge and his family arrived in Austin's Colony in 1826. Austin granted Hodge one of the leagues he had reserved for himself. Hodge's Bend was situated on the road running from Fort Bend to Harrisburg and was a gathering place for family and friends alike.

Source:
Marguerite Crain #30

"You, in Kentucky, cannot for a moment conceive of the beauty of one of our prairies in the spring. Imagine for yourself a vast plain extending as far as the eye can reach, with nothing but the deep blue sky to bound the prospect, excepting on the east side where runs a broad red stream, with lofty trees rearing themselves upon its banks, and you have our prairie. This is covered with a carpet of the richest verdure, from the midst of which spring up wild flowers of every hue and shade, rendering the scene one of almost fairy-like beauty. Indeed it is impossible to step without crushing these fairest of nature's works. Upon these natural flower gardens feed numerous herds of buffalo, deer, and other wild animals. Here and there may be seen beautiful clumps of trees, and anon, a little thicket comes in view. The flowers of the prairie are certainly the most beautiful which I have ever beheld. Our ladies in Kentucky would feel themselves amply repaid for all the labor which they bestow upon their beautiful flower gardens, could they but afford one half of the beauty of one of our prairies.

Yours, truly,
W.B.D."

—from *Letters From an Early Settler of Texas*
by William B. Dewees

GEORGE HUFF

George Huff, a blacksmith and mechanic in Austin's Colony, was born in 1781 in Wilkinson County, Mississippi. He shows up in 1811 as a resident of neighboring Amite County.

Huff received one and one-half leagues occupying either side of Bernard and Peach creeks in present Fort Bend and Wharton counties. The extra land may have been awarded because of Huff's agreement to build a sawmill and grist mill. In the first census of Texas, Huff is listed as between forty and fifty years of age. His wife (not named, but believed to be Mary) is of the same age. Also listed in his household are two males, aged seven to sixteen, one male, sixteen to twenty-five, and two females, also sixteen to twenty-five. One of his sons, Jacob, preceded the rest of the family to Austin's Colony in order to clear and prepare the land. Jacob died in 1833.

By 1825, George Huff had constructed a sawmill on the property. He opened a store in San Felipe de Austin with his son William. In 1835 he was in charge of provisions sent to the headquarters of the Texian volunteer force at Gonzales.

George Huff is listed on the 1840 tax roll in Austin County as owning eight town lots, four slaves, a horse, and a gold watch. He died before 1850.

Source:
Joyce Gray Clegg Robinson #440

DR. JOHNSON CALHOUN HUNTER

J ohnson Calhoun Hunter was born May 22, 1787, in Charleston, South Carolina. There, Hunter married Martha Harbert of Wythe County, Virginia. After receiving a diploma in medicine, Hunter moved first to southeastern Ohio and then to new Madrid, Missouri. In 1820 or 1821, Hunter joined an expedition that traveled to San Antonio, where he had dealings with the Veramendi family.

Hunter decided to relocate in Texas, and attempted to take his family there by way of water from New Orleans. They were shipwrecked on an island, where they remained until rescued by a passing vessel. Hunter was granted land by the Mexican government at Morgan's Point on Galveston Bay, and there he built his first Texas home.

In 1829 the Hunters moved to Fort Bend County. Hunter's Plantation, outside of Richmond, lay on Oyster Creek and at the edge of the prairie. In early 1836, the Hunters abandoned their home in advance of Santa Anna's invading army, driving their cattle herd. Their route brought them close to the Battle of San Jacinto.

They returned to the plantation, which had been temporarily occupied by the Mexican troops. Dr. Hunter died there on May 29, 1855.

Between 1811 and 1836, the Hunters had thirteen children: Jacob, Robert Hancock, Mary, John Calhoun, Harriet Harbert, Thomas Jefferson, Thaddeus Warsaw, Messina, Martha, Latisia, William, Amanda Wilson Calhoun, and Walter Crockett.

Source:
Louise Schoener #197

SAMUEL ISAACKS

At seventeen years of age, Samuel Isaacks was on the Brazos River with his friend William Andrews when Stephen F. Austin brought the first colonists there in December 1821. He was included in Austin's Old Three Hundred.

Isaacks returned to Louisiana, where he married Nancy Allen. They had two sons, but Nancy died in 1828. He remarried and is shown in records with his second wife Martha (Patsy) Richardson and their children. Also shown is the eldest son of the first marriage, William.

Samuel enlisted in the Jasper Volunteers. He received several grants of land and also a veteran pension for himself and wife Martha for his service in the Texas Revolution.

About 1850 he secured land at Lynchburg, adjacent to the San Jacinto Battleground. He established a freight line between Coldsprings and Lynchburg. He stayed there until after the Civil War, when he sold his property and moved to Taylor's Bayou in Seabrook, where he lived until his death in 1878.

Samuel Isaacks' grandson writes:

> As I remember him, he was probably six feet tall, raw-boned, or stalwart, and very active for a man of more than 72 years old. . . . His wife, Martha . . . small of stature, probably never balancing the scales at as much as 100 pounds, she was one of the most kindly and motherly souls . . . She smoked a clay pipe, and my greatest delight was to help her fill and light it.

Source:
Betty J. Moczygemba #264

ISAAC JACKSON, SR.

There has been no record found of the birthplace of Isaac Jackson, Sr. (1771-1846). However, he appears in the first census of Greene County, Georgia, in 1790, where a younger brother, Henry, was born in 1797.

Isaac and his wife, Elizabeth, had five children: Isaac C., James, John, Job, and Nancy (Pollard). In 1824, Isaac Sr. received a league of land on the east side of the Brazos River in present Grimes County, opposite the town of Washington. He was first listed as a family man in Texas, but Elizabeth may never have joined him. She is listed in the 1850 Greene County census as age seventy, living with her son Isaac C. Later records in Texas list Isaac, Sr., as a single farmer and stockraiser.

Proof that Isaac, Sr., took part in the Texas Revolution is the award of another league of land, this one in Caldwell County, for being permanently disabled in that conflict. He died in 1846 and was buried in present Grimes County. Although he probably never saw the Caldwell County grant, sons Isaac C. and James came to Texas from Georgia and claimed it in 1861.

Source:
Joy Mellie Gooch Dotson #383

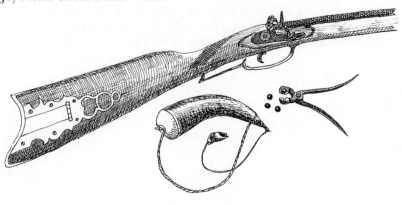

44

HENRY JONES

Henry Jones was born March 15, 1789, in Madison County, Virginia, near "Blue Ridge." He married Nancy Stiles on January 31, 1821. Early in 1822, they came to Texas with Austin's Old Three Hundred colonists. They first settled in Washington County, near Independence. Later that year, Henry Jones traveled to what is now Fort Bend County. There he selected a league of land, just below present day Richmond.

Henry and Nancy built their home on the prairie. Their children were William, James, Mary Moore (Polly), John Henry, Nettie Ellen, Virginia Claudine, Ruth, Elizabeth, Vivian Ann, Susan (Sudie), Wiley Powell, Nancy Timelia, Emily Laura, Henry, and Thomas Walter.

Henry Jones was responsible for the first road to East and West Columbia. He also served on the first grand jury held in Fort Bend County.

In the 1850 Fort Bend County census, Henry's real estate

had a value of almost $32,000. In the 1860 census, he was listed as seventy-three years of age, a farmer whose real estate was valued at $193,999 and his personal property at $96,000.

Nancy died August 5, 1851. When Henry died in June 8, 1861, intestate, his possessions were listed as forty-five slaves, several hundred hogs and horses, 4,344 acres of land, valued at $162,862.50, and 1,110 acres of land, including a homestead, valued at $15,165.

Henry and Nancy Jones are buried in Jones Cemetery, located on the George Ranch, near Richmond.

Source:
Virginia Scarborough #160

★　★　★

Dilue Rose Harris records that just after the fall of the Alamo, a large herd of buffaloes came by—three or four thousand of them. They crossed the Brazos River above Fort Bend and came out of the bottom at Stafford's Point, making their first appearance before day. They passed in sight of the Rose house, but folks could see only a dark cloud of dust, which looked like a sandstorm. As the night was very dark no one could tell when the last buffalo passed. The buffaloes went on to the coast, and the prairie looked afterwards as if it had been plowed.

★　★　★

46

JAMES WALES JONES

James Wales Jones was born January 13, 1797, in Columbia County, Georgia. He joined Austin's Colony in January 1822. He settled in what is now Wharton County. He received one *sitio* of land in the rich bottomland of the Brazos River, and a *labor* in what is now Fort Bend County.

Jones married Hetty Stiles on August 24, 1825, in the Fort Settlement. They later had to be married by the Catholic church, in accordance with Mexican law. They had the following children: Ann Elizabeth, William Thomas, Robert Ellis, James Randall, Stephen Austin, Richard Henry, John Stiles, James Walter, and Polly White Jones.

James Wales and Hetty Jones built a home near present-day Richmond on the Brazos River and called it "Jones Heights." In 1835, when the colonies began their revolt against the Mexican government, James Wales joined the company of Capt. Wiley Martin, who was ordered by Gen. Sam Houston to defend the ferry at Thompson's Crossing on the Brazos. James Wales was granted a bounty grant certificate for 320 acres of land in Atascosa County for his service in the Army of the Republic of Texas, from July 8, 1835, to June 7, 1836.

James Wales Jones died September 29, 1847, from pneumonia. He was buried in a family cemetery in Prairie Lea, Texas. Hetty Stiles Jones lived to be ninety-one. Her death date was April 9, 1899. She, too, was buried in the family plot. Both bodies were later moved to the State Cemetery in Austin.

Source:
Rebecca B. Lee #130

CAPT. RANDALL JONES

Randall Jones was born August 19, 1786, in Columbia County, Georgia, son of Thomas and second wife, Sarah Story Smith.

Randall and brother James arrived in San Felipe in January 1822. A year's search provided a suitable location on the Brazos River bend near present Richmond. In January 1823 land was cleared and cabins erected. Randall received a Spanish title to a league and a *labor* which was patented July 15, 1824. He went back to Louisiana and returned with Fort Bend's first large shipment of stock.

On October 11, 1824, Randall married Mary (Polly) Andrews (Andrus), daughter of William and Susan Andrews, in a "bond ceremony" performed by Stephen F. Austin. Father Michael Muldoon performed a formal ceremony on June 3, 1831. Nine children were born to Randall and Polly Jones: Wiley Martin, James Austin, Martha, Pamelia Ann, Sudie E., Sam Houston, James Miller, Eliza M., and Sallie C.

His service to Texas was long and varied. He participated in the Anahuac Expedition in 1832, was a member of the General Consultation of 1835-1836 and of the *ayuntamiento* of San Felipe, and served in the Texas Army 1835-1837 and again in 1842 during the second Mexican invasion. He received a bounty warrant for 320 acres for that service.

Polly Andrews Jones died on April 17, 1861, and Randall died in Houston at the home of his son-in-law, Gustave Cook, on June 3, 1873.

They were buried on the Jones *labor*, but their remains and those of their daughter, Martha Jones Beale, were removed to the State Cemetery, Austin. The gravesites are C-AO 5 and C-AO 4.

Source:
Mrs. Leslie B. Duncan #83

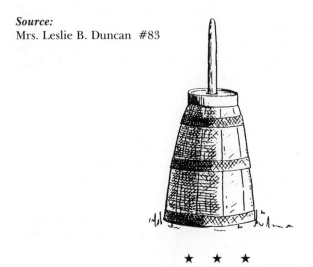

". . . *In short, my mottoes have been*—The redemption of Texas from the wilderness, Fidelity and gratitude to my adopted country, and to be inflexibly true to the interests and just rights of my settlers. *It is my boast to say that I have never deviated from these general principles, and it is a matter of proud gratification to me that my colony has always possessed the confidence of this Govt. . . .*"

—From Austin's letter to Thomas F. Leaming

★   ★   ★

BARZILLAI KUYKENDALL

Barzillai Kuykendall came to Texas as an adult with his father, Abner.

Barzillai received title to a *labor* of land in Austin County, about six miles north of San Felipe. A second tract was received on April 27, 1824, a one-fourth league located about six miles west of Bellville. Barzillai farmed, raised cattle, and fought the Indians.

Barzillai married a cousin, Katherine Kuykendall, in 1828. Their children were Lucinda, Martha, Sarah, and Joseph. Lucinda, the youngest daughter, was born in 1840, and Katherine died soon after. Barzillai next married a woman named Elizabeth, about 1847-48. They had three children.

On February 5, 1836, Barzillai received another three-fourth league of land in what is now Lee County, between Giddings and Manheim.

During the Battle of San Jacinto, Barzillai was a member of the company of his brother, Capt. Gibson Kuykendall. They were to guard the baggage and to care for the wounded at Harrisburg.

The 1860 and 1870 census reports show Barzillai was a farmer. These same records show that he, Elizabeth, and their children, Solomon, William H., and Nancy (Nannie), lived in Evergreen, Lee County, on a league of land which was granted to his father, Abner Kuykendall.

Barzillai died March 31, 1873, and Elizabeth died April 10, 1873.

Source:
Orrell Lee Patrick, Jr. #320

ROBERT H. KUYKENDALL

Robert H. Kuykendall (1790-1830) was the son of Adam and Margaret (Hardin) Kuykendall, probably born near Princeton, Kentucky. About 1814, Robert married Sarah Ann Gilleland, daughter of William and Nancy (Johnson) Gilleland of Davidson County, Tennessee.

In the fall of 1821, the Kuykendalls, relatives, and friends moved into the Spanish province of Texas, reaching the Brazos River in November. On January 1, 1822, Robert, brother-in-law Daniel Gilleland, and others proceeded to the east bank of the Colorado and settled at what became Beason's Landing. Under colonial organization, Robert was chosen as captain of militia for the district. He led colonists into several Indian battles between 1822 and 1824.

On July 16, 1824, Robert Kuykendall received two leagues of land along the Colorado. Stephen F. Austin wrote that Kuykendall deserved the larger grant "because he has a large family, was one of the FIRST settlers, and has always protected the other settlers from the Savage Indians."

In 1826 Captain Kuykendall incurred an injury in an Indian fight which led to blindness and paralysis despite doctors' efforts. He died and presumably lies in the old cemetery at Matagorda.

Robert and Sarah had six children to survive infancy: R.H. or "Gill," Mary or "Molly," Jane, Joseph Felix (died young), and Albert and Thomas (twins). Sarah Gilleland Kuykendall died in Matagorda County in 1857 and is buried in the Hawley Cemetery near Blessing.

Source:
Marshall E. Kuykendall #29

JOEL LEAKEY

Ann Hadley, born March 24, 1754, the daughter of Simon and Bridget Hadley of Surry County, North Carolina, married Thomas Leakey, born June 16, 1751. They had three children: Simon, born August 8, 1778; Joel, born March 1, 1780; and Lydia, born September 16, 1793.

At the age of nineteen, Joel helped Samuel Calloway and others build roads in the county. He and Samuel's daughter, Nancy, were married in 1799 and were parents of a son, Thomas, born about 1800. Thomas died in 1861 in Walker County, Texas. Joel and Nancy also had seven daughters: Leny, Mary Asenith, Elizabeth, Lydia, Anna, Nancy, and Ruth.

Sometime after 1804, Joel and his family left Surry County and moved to Natchitoches Parish, Louisiana, in February of 1819. He had 640 acres on the waters of Negrite Bayou. He made a home for his family there until he came to Texas and joined Stephen F. Austin's Colony.

The Leakey family proceeded to build a permanent home near the Brazos on the present Austin-Washington County lines. From all reports, Joel was a very hospitable, caring man who helped his neighbors build ferries, welcomed travelers, and made his home available to engaged couples when a traveling priest could perform marriages. He was one of the most influential men in the colony.

Source:
Ruth T. Foiles #80

WILLIAM LITTLE

William Little, a native of Pennsylvania, was born circa 1790. As a youth, he came south, and served as captain of a Mississippi River steamboat. He married Jane Edwards, a native of Tennessee.

William Little heard about free land in Texas. He met with fourteen other men and made the journey to Natchitoches, Louisiana, to meet with Stephen F. Austin and Commissioner Don Erasmo Smith. They left Natchitoches on July 5, 1821. In San Antonio they met with Governor Martinez, who recognized Stephen Austin as successor of his father's rights. This group looked at the land along the Guadalupe, Lavaca, Navidad, Colorado, Brazos and San Jacinto rivers, as well as the Gulf Coast. Austin decided this would be the site for his first colony.

They returned to Louisiana and bought a schooner, the *Lively*, loaded the boats with implements, food, guns, ammunition, and other supplies. William Little was in charge of the little thirty-foot sailboat. With about twenty passengers, they left New Orleans on November 25, 1821.

William Little received his grant of one league and one *labor* July 10, 1824, on the east side of the Brazos River, about twelve miles below the present town of Richmond. There William and Jane Edwards Little reared a large family. Their children were as follows: John, William, Walter W., Martha Jane, Louisa, James K., Robert, and George.

William Little died at his home on July 8, 1841.

Sources:
Virginia Davis Scarborough #160
Antoinette Davis Reading #161

NATHANIEL LYNCH

Nathaniel Lynch was born in New York state in 1786. He married Frances Hubert, also of New York state. They had two sons born in New York, Franklin and William. Before 1820, they migrated to the Missouri Territory, where Elizabeth was born circa 1820. Another son was born to the Lynches in Texas in 1824.

Nathaniel and his family came to Texas in 1822. He was granted a league and a *labor* of land, which lay on each side of the San Jacinto River. Lynch had operated a ferry back in Missouri and he soon established one across the San Jacinto. He did not apply for a license to operate publicly until 1830. During the Runaway Scrape in 1836, hundreds crossed his ferry to escape Santa Anna.

Lynch built a double hewed log structure, which housed his family, a store, and a tavern. He platted the towns of Lynchburg and San Jacinto. He was postmaster of Lynchburg and was appointed second municipal judge of Harrisburg. During the Revolution, he served three months in the Texas Army, despite his age. He received a land grant for his service.

In business with David G. Burnet, Lynch is said to have built the first steam-operated sawmill in Texas. In 1973 parts of the old mill were found in the underbrush at the San Jacinto State Park.

Frances Hubert Lynch sewed the Flag of Independence for Capt. William Scott's Lynchburg Volunteers, when they marched for the Siege of Bexar. Some historians believe it may have been the first Lone Star flag.

In the first census of Austin's Colony, Nathaniel Lynch was listed as a carpenter, farmer, and stockraiser. Lynch died February 14, 1837, and is buried in the old Lynchburg Cemetery.

Source:
Flossie Stanley Keels #131

SHUBAEL MARSH

Shubael Marsh (1797?-1868) was raised by his parents, Shubael and Elizabeth (Foxcroft) March, in Portland, Maine. Tradition says that all of this large family, except for young Shubael, remained in the East.

After coming to Texas from Hannibal, Missouri, where he had taught school, Marsh took an oath of loyalty to Mexico in April 1824 and received a league of land in present Brazoria County on July 8. He was a merchant in Brazoria for several years. The census of March 1826 lists him as a single man, between twenty-five and forty years of age.

As *sindico procurador*, Marsh presided over an election at Bolivar. He married Lucinda Pitts and they later moved to her family's neighborhood in present Washington County.

In 1835 Marsh applied for another grant. Stephen F. Austin, in supporting the request, wrote: "I shall state that the applicant was one of the first immigrants to this country, and . . . he is a man of good customs, honesty and much industry, and I believe that he has sufficient capital to settle and cultivate the tract he solicits. . . ."

Marsh ultimately owned land in many parts of the state. He died at age seventy-one at the home he built near Independence, with its flower and vegetable gardens and fruit orchards. His granddaughter, Margaret Hall Hicks, wrote extensively about Marsh from personal recollections (see references).

Sources:
Genevieve Hicks Coonly #357
Jean Hicks Richey #356

ARTHUR McCORMICK

Arthur McCormick, with his wife Margaret and two sons, Michael and John, emigrated from Ireland to America in 1818 and in that year located in New Orleans. From there they went to Texas in 1822 and located in Harris County on land that afterwards became known as the Arthur McCormick League and *labor*. He was an early associate of Stephen F. Austin, who persuaded McCormick to consent to return to Ireland and to bring out a colony of Irish emigrants.

In February 1825 he visited Austin in San Felipe to receive the necessary papers and credentials for carrying out the project. On returning to his home and in crossing Buffalo Bayou near Harrisburg, it was necessary for him to swim. He was caught in a thicket of grapevines and was drowned, as was his horse. The widow resided on the home place with her sons until she died some years later.

The McCormick league of land was situated on the west bank of the San Jacinto River, the place where Santa Anna and his army were defeated on April 21, 1836. When Margaret found her land covered with dead Mexican soldiers, she went to Gen. Sam Houston and asked him to remove the stinking corpses. Houston replied, "Why, Lady, your land will be famed in history as the spot where the glorious battle was fought." Margaret was left with the problem to solve of getting the dead Mexicans buried.

Source:
June McCormick Gaume #534

JOHN McCROSKY

Scot-Irishman John McCrosky, the son of James and Susan Walker McCrosky, was born November 15, 1792, in Scott County, Kentucky. He came to Texas in 1821 as a tanner and one of Stephen F. Austin's colonists. He received two leagues and a *labor* of land in Brazoria, Colorado, and Austin counties on August 16, 1824.

His original one-story double log cabin, built in Brazoria County in 1824, now restored, is the oldest log cabin in Texas today. McCrosky sold the Brazoria County property to John Williams in 1825 and moved his tannery to Colorado County. There he married Sarah Ann Bright, widow of Eli Hunter, in 1829. She was the daughter of David and Judith Bright, also colonists. Their son, William Hart McCrosky, was born May 9, 1830, in Colorado County.

McCrosky's tannery established on the Colorado River near Columbus was one of the first industries in Texas. A member of the first Texas Rangers in the Colorado District, he was listed in Moses Morrison's Company as a corporal, age thirty, farmer and courier. He was elected third lieutenant of a company of militia at San Felipe de Austin on July 10, 1824. In January 1827 McCrosky met with other settlers at the home of Bartlett Sims to adopt resolutions and to condemn the Fredonian Rebellion.

John McCrosky died about December 1831, and is believed to be buried on his property near the tannery. In 1832 Sarah Ann McCrosky married William D. Lacey, who had worked for John McCrosky at the tannery. Lacey was one of the signers of the Texas Declaration of Independence.

Source:
Donna McCrosky Johnson #23

JOHN H. MOORE

John H. Moore was born in Sumner County, Tennessee, on August 13, 1800. At age eighteen, he ran away from Transylvania College, in Lexington, Kentucky. His father made him go back, but he again left school and went to Texas in 1821. He fought the Indians in the upper Colorado area and in 1824 secured a land grant from Stephen F. Austin. He and Thomas Gray received title to a league of land in Brazoria County, and a *labor* in Colorado County.

John H. Moore and Eliza Cummins, born April 23, 1803, whom he married on June 14, 1827, made their first home in Columbus. Later they moved to present LaGrange. Their children were William Bowen, Tabitha B., Eliza, John Henry, Jr., Robert J., and Mary E.

Moore built a twin blockhouse on his plantation, which was known as Moore's Fort. He organized and named Fayette County, and gave the land for the town of LaGrange.

It is known that Moore owned one hundred slaves; when they were freed, most of them stayed with the Moore family.

Moore was a patriot and an advocate of the independence of Texas. There are numerous accounts of the "Come and Take It" flag which he is attributed to have signed. Austin ordered him to organize a cavalry and Moore was elected colonel of the volunteer army, becoming the commander of the Battle of Gonzales. He then returned to the United States for financial aid and reinforcements. Moore died at LaGrange on December 2, 1880, and is buried on the plantation. Eliza died February 25, 1877.

Sources:
Kathleen Fisk Hale #355
Donna McCrosky Johnson #23

WILLIAM MORTON

William Morton arrived in Texas in 1822. He had sailed from Mobile, Alabama, with his wife, Jane, and five children. The family was shipwrecked near present-day Galveston and joined the members of the *Lively* expedition, which followed the Brazos upstream.

Morton settled in what is now Fort Bend County, on the east side of the Brazos River. As one of the original "Old Three Hundred," he received one and one-half leagues and one *labor* of land in Fort Bend County. Morton was a brick mason, farmer, and cattleraiser. As a brick mason he was authorized to plan an academy at San Felipe. He was also commissioned to build the jail there.

Morton was a member of the Masonic Lodge. The Morton Lodge No. 72, chartered January 24, 1851, located in Richmond, was named after him. William Morton drowned in the Brazos River in 1833 while attempting to cross the flooded river. His body was never recovered.

One of the Morton girls married William Little. Daughter Marian (Mary) married William P. Huff. She was baptized by Father Michael Muldoon. Her baptism certificate is on file at the Center for American History, University of Texas, Austin.

Source:
Mrs. W. T. Robinson, Jr. #440

JOSEPH NEWMAN

Joseph Newman's land grant was No. 57 and it was received on August 10, 1824. It consisted of one league on the east bank of the Colorado River near present-day Egypt, in Wharton County, and a *labor* on the Brazos River, near San Felipe de Austin.

The earliest documentation on Joseph Newman is his marriage at age nineteen to sixteen-year-old Rachel Rabb, daughter of William Rabb, on June 21, 1806, in Warren County, Ohio. From Ohio, the Rabbs and Newmans moved to Illinois Territory, and by 1820 they had moved to what was known as the Jonesborough settlement, now in Red River County, Texas.

Problems soon arose in this area. Officials in Miller County, Arkansas, tried to collect taxes from the settlers and to govern them while the settlers on the south side of Red River believed themselves to be in Spanish Territory. In 1821 William Rabb wrote a letter to the Spanish governor of Texas, complaining about the situation. This letter was accompanied by a petition (or memorial) from Pecan Point settlement. The people there were asking that the Spanish government send a commandant and an *alcalde* to govern the settlement. In the event this was not possible, they asked permission to select someone to fill these offices. The petition, known as the "Joseph Newman Memorial," carried the signatures of about eighty settlers.

The Rabbs and Joseph Newman received land grants in Austin's Colony in 1824. Joseph Newman's grant adjoined that of his brother-in-law, Andrew Rabb.

Joseph Newman lived only about six years after settling in the colony. In his last will and testament, signed on February 15, 1831, he requested to be buried in the cemetery on his property. His will left his property to his wife Rachel Rabb Newman and their children, namely: Mary, William, Eliza, Minerva, Sally, Elizabeth, Thomas, Ali, Joseph, Jr., and Andrew. The three youngest sons were born in Austin's Colony. Andrew Rabb was named executor and Rachel Newman, executrix, of Joseph's estate.

Source:
Coleman C. Newman #116

"... Quite unexpectedly, as it were, a report has reached the public ear, that the country lying west of the Sabine river, is a tract of surpassing beauty, exceeding even our best western lands in productiveness, with a climate perfectly salubrious, and of a temperature, at all seasons of the year, most delightful. The admirers of this new country ... are not content, in their descriptions of it, to make use of ordinary terms of commendation. They hesitate not to call it a splendid country—an enchanting spot. It would seem as if enchantment had, indeed, thrown its spell over their minds, for, with very few exceptions, all who return from this fairy land, are perfect enthusiasts in their admiration of it ..."

—Mary Austin Holley, 1831 and 1836

GEORGE SAMUEL PENTECOST

George Samuel Pentecost and his wife Marta Ellen left their home in Alabama to join the original colonists of Stephen F. Austin, acquiring a *sitio* of land, in August 1824, in present Matagorda County.

Dissatisfied with the first homesite near the Colorado River and with a second homesite near the San Bernard River, Pentecost established a flourishing plantation in Big Creek Community in Fort Bend County, on land purchased from Samuel Pharr, husband of daughter Lucy Pentecost.

Pentecost had been a resident of Monroe County, Alabama, prior to the War of 1812 and served with the Mississippi Volunteers during this war, as did two brothers of Martha Dentley Pentecost, James and John Dentley.

In 1827 Pentecost was opposed to the Fredonian Rebellion and declared loyalty to the Mexican government. He later joined the calls for independence and a son, George Washington Pentecost, was among the heroes at the Battle of San Jacinto, along with a son-in-law, Andrew Jackson Beard, husband of Sally Pentecost.

George S. Pentecost is buried in the Brown Cemetery near Big Creek, having passed away in 1841 in the fiftieth year of life. His wife, Martha, is thought to be buried at the second homesite near the San Bernard River.

Children named in his will were: Lucy Ellen, Gracey Elizabeth, George Washington, Mary Jane, James Denley, Sara (Sally) Jane, Susan Evelyn, and William Walter.

Sources:
Sally Brumbelow Bell #422
Esther Beard

DR. JAMES AENEAS PHELPS

Dr. James Aeneas Phelps was born in Grandy, Connecticut, in 1793. After college, he moved to Wilkinson County, Mississippi, where he was listed in the 1820 census. He married Rosetta Adeline Yerby on April 18, 1821.

Dr. Phelps came to Texas on the *Lively*, as one of Stephen F. Austin's Old Three Hundred Colonists. He received a league of land and two *labors*, on the Brazos River, in what is now Brazoria County.

Dr. Phelps built a large two-story house for his family and named his plantation "Orozimbo." The house stood about ten miles northeast of present-day West Columbia.

In March 1835, six Master Masons—Phelps, John A. Wharton, Asa Brigham, Alexander Russell, Anson Jones, and James P. Campbell—met in Brazoria to establish a lodge. Although it was forbidden under the Mexican law, they signed a petition to the Grand Lodge of Louisiana. Holland Lodge No. 36. U.D., opened on December 27, 1835, with Dr. Phelps as treasurer.

On March 19, 1836, Dr. Phelps and Dr. Anson Jones left Brazoria to join the army. Dr. Phelps was attached to the medical staff during the Battle of San Jacinto. After Santa Anna was captured, he was a prisoner at Orozimbo, from July to November of 1836.

In 1842 Santa Anna showed his gratitude to Dr. Phelps, when their oldest son Orlando was captured in the ill-fated Mier Expedition. During the drawing of the black beans, Santa Anna heard the name Phelps mentioned. He saved the young man's life and sent him home.

Dr. Phelps' will was probated on November 9, 1847, and he is buried at Orozimbo. In 1936 the State of Texas erected two monuments at the site.

Source:
A. Frederick Renaud #235

JOSEPH HENRY POLLEY

The adventurous Joseph Henry Polley left home in Whitehall, New York, at age fifteen. He was a teamster at seventeen in the War of 1812. At the close of the war he immigrated to Missouri.

In 1820 Polley joined Moses Austin for a look at Texas. In 1824 he received a 4,587-acre grant of land from Stephen F. Austin near Richmond.

Polley competed patiently with Stephen F. Austin for the hand of Pollie Bailey, the daughter of Brit Bailey, another Old Three Hundred colonist. His persistence won out and soon they were married.

Polley served several terms as sheriff of Brazoria District. He also was a farmer, rancher, and in the freighting business in Brazoria. At the time of his demise in 1859 his herds were the most extensive in Texas.

In October of 1836 the meeting of the first Congress of Texas was held in Joseph and Pollie's home. The question of creating a seal was posed. Henry Smith, the provisional governor, was wearing a coat with buttons displaying a single star. It was decided that the star would be an appropriate symbol for the flag and seal.

Polley and his wife, in 1847, moved to the Cibolo Valley in what is now Wilson County, where he constructed a permanent home. They are buried there in a family plot.

Source:
George B. Everts #196

May 29th 1829

"D. G. Burnet Esq.

N. B. This splendid City 'en embrio' has been born since your departure. It is on the Brasos river about 25 miles up from the mouth by water—Sam Williams has a fine daughter—he goes in to New Orleans tomorrow with Cap John Austin—Parker has a fine daughter—J. H. Bell has been very sick with the Rheumatism, tho he has another fine boy—in short this has been quite a prolific season amongst the Ladies and it is truly gratifying to say that I never saw healthier children in my life—Miss Sarah Cummins married Mr. Dennet a short time since in *defiance* of the old woman her mother who is *very* wrathy—you know she has made a rule to *discard* every child who marries right or wrong—Sarah did right as I think—

—S. F. Austin"

WILLIAM PRYOR

William Pryor was one of Stephen F. Austin's Old Three Hundred colonists but received his Mexican land grant somewhat uniquely. He received his first *labor* of land on August 24, 1824. It lay on the east bank of the Brazos River directly across from the town of San Felipe de Austin. He received his league in Washington County in 1828. Estevan (Stephen) F. Austin and the Baron de Bastrop signed it.

William Pryor was born about 1780 to Joseph Pryor and Mary Fleming in Botetourt County, Virginia. He married Betsy Green Trammell about 1808. They had eleven children, six of whom survived to adulthood: Althea Laura, Trammell, Mary, Harriet, Rosannah, and Elizabeth. In 1826 Harriet married Noel F. Roberts, another of the Old Three Hundred families. In 1834 Elizabeth married Noel's son William by a previous marriage. Both marriages produced children, thus combining two Old Three Hundred families.

William Barret Travis noted in his diary that he "sat with old Pryor" on September 9 and attended his funeral the next day in San Felipe de Austin. Thus we know that William died on September 9, 1833, leaving a remarkable will that contains an abundance of family information. William Pryor disowned his only son in the will because he "stained my honor and seized without my leave and dissipated my property." He left his estate to his five daughters. The will was somehow lost for seventeen years during the revolution and the years of the Republic. It was written under Mexican rule, was continued during the Republic of Texas, and was finally probated in 1850 after Texas became a state.

Source:
James Edgar Roberts #488

JOHN RABB

John Rabb was born December 31, 1798, in Fayette County, Pennsylvania. He settled in Miller County, Arkansas, at a young age. In 1823 he moved to Texas with his wife, Mary Crownover Rabb; his son; his father, William; his brothers, Andrew and Thomas; and his sister, Rachel, together with Rachel's husband, Joseph Newman, and family.

All of the men received land grants from the Mexican government through Stephen F. Austin as they were members of the first 300 families.

John Rabb and family spent most of their lives in and around LaGrange. He built one of the first grist mills in Texas. As a bonus for the enterprise he received a league of land.

John Rabb is known as the first Methodist convert in Austin's Colony. He was one of the founders of Rutersville College in Rutersville, Texas.

On August 10, 1860, he decided to sell his grist mill and placed the following advertisement in the LaGrange paper and in *Harper's New Monthly Magazine*:

> Can't get the kind of miller I want. Won't have any other sort. Too pushing a business for an old man. Can't get time to pray enough. Too far from Church. Intend, by the will of God, to sell out and quit business. A good flouring, corn and shingling

Mary Crownover Rabb wrote that when she was in her first house in Texas, Andrew Rabb made a spinning wheel for her. She was very pleased and got to work making clothes for her family. She would pick cotton with her fingers and spin "600 thread around the reel everyday." When she was lonely and frightened, "I kept my new spinning wheel whisling all day and a good part of the night for while the wheel was rowering it would keep me from hearing the Indians walking around hunting mischieaf."

mill for sale!! (Steam Power) With large quantity of cedar timber and any amount of land, from one hundred to four thousand acres. For sale on reasonable terms. Ten miles North of LaGrange, Fayette County, Texas. Aug. 10, 1860.

In 1860 he moved with his wife to Travis County and settled at Barton Springs, in present-day Austin, where he died on June 5, 1861.

Source:
Lillian Bell Rabb #129

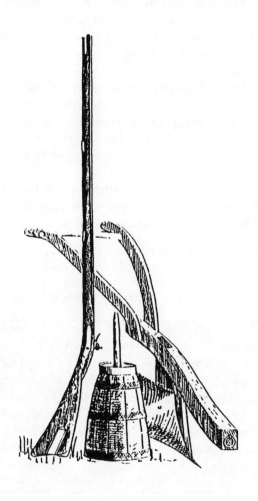

CAPT. THOMAS J. RABB

"Captain Rabb was known in Texas as a gentleman, scholar, husband, father, and Christian. . . ." Thus reads a newspaper obituary for Thomas Rabb, a Fayette County, Pennsylvania, native born around 1795 to William and Mary (Smalley) Rabb and one of several family members who were Old Three Hundred grantees.

The Rabbs arrived in the Austin Colony area by December 1821. The following year, William and Thomas accompanied Stephen F. Austin as far as Bexar on Austin's trip to Mexico City to confirm his colonization contract. In 1824 the Rabb clan settled near present-day Egypt in Wharton County. That same year, Thomas received a one-league grant and was also named first lieutenant in the colony militia.

In October 1835, the opening days of the Texas Revolution, Thomas joined the Texian army. He took part in the Battle of Mission Concepcion; soon after, he was assigned by the General Council of Texas to recruit for the army. As a result, Thomas was not able to take part in the Texas Declaration of Independence even though he had been chosen as the delegate from Mina.

Capt. Thomas Rabb led his volunteers into Gonzales on the day the Alamo fell. The unit became Company F, First Regiment, Texas Volunteer Army.

In 1840 Thomas served as captain of Rangers in a decisive victory over the Comanches, and again in 1842 to meet a Mexican raid on San Antonio. He died in Fayette County, Texas, in 1846.

Thomas and his first wife, Serena (Gilbert), had Ulysses, Sarah, and Mary Louisa. After Serena's death in 1836, Thomas and second wife Barthenia (maiden name unknown) had Adelia Ann and Angeline Thomas.

Source:
Col. Victor C. Wegenhoft, USAF (Ret.), #114

WILLIAM RABB

William Rabb was born in Fayette County, Pennsylvania, on December 27, 1770. He married Mary Scott. Later he married Mary (Polly) Smalley. It is not known whether his five children, Rachel, Andrew, John, Thomas and Ulysses, were children from the first or second marriage.

This family came to Texas as a member of Austin's Old Three Hundred colonists, about December 15, 1823. They settled on Colorado River, near the present town of LaGrange. The place was known as Indian Hills at the time.

William Rabb erected a gristmill and a sawmill on the Colorado River. All the materials came from New Orleans, except the millstones, which were shipped from Scotland.

The first census of Austin's Colony lists William Rabb as a farmer and stockraiser, over fifty years of age, with a wife, one son, and one slave.

William Rabb died ca. 1832, at the age of sixty-two. His wife Mary (Polly) died soon after. Rabb's Creek in Lee County and Rabb's Prairie, a farming community, were named for him. They are near LaGrange.

Sources:
Irene T. Philips #172
Mrs. John Wayne Reedy #214
Mark Edward Robinson #213

William Rabb was given five *sitios* and two *labors* of land in Austin's Colony on the condition that he build and operate a gristmill. They were unable to build for a few years because of Indian raids. When it was time to build, William Rabb ordered the equipment from New Orleans, except the buhrs or grinding stones. They came from Scotland by ship to Matagorda Bay. It would have been impossible to move the heavy stones in a conventional manner since there were no good roads. Rabb constructed an axle from a tree, mounted the stones as wheels, hitched his teams of oxen, and rolled the stones to the site more than 100 miles away.

ELIJAH ROARK

Elijah Roark was born in North Carolina circa 1785-88. He moved to Missouri Territory circa 1810. He married Cynthia Fisher circa 1812. While living in the Missouri Territory, three of their children were born.

In 1821, Elijah learned that Stephen F. Austin was enlisting families to move to Texas. Records show that the Roark family was in the colony on October 13, 1822. The family lived on Oyster Creek in Fort Bend County. On July 10, 1824, Elijah received title to a league and a *labor* of land. Twin daughters were born to them there. In all, there were seven children: Leo, Andrew Jackson, Rebecca, twins Lucinda and Louisa, Andy, and Mary, who was born a few months after Elijah was murdered by Indians.

In 1829 Elijah, his son Leo, and a friend loaded a wagon and, driving the hogs, began the long trip to San Antonio, about two hundred miles. They had crossed the Guadalupe River and made camp for the night when they were attacked by Indians. Elijah and his friend were murdered, but Leo escaped in the underbrush. He made his way to San Antonio, where he told of the attack. He and others went back to the scene of the campsite, where they found the two men scalped and their wagon burned. The Indians had taken their stock. Wolves were eating on the corpses—a very gruesome picture.

Cynthia Roark died on December 25, 1836.

Source:
Doris Ballard Drake #272

NOEL FRANCIS ROBERTS

Noel F. Roberts, one of Stephen F. Austin's Old Three Hundred colonists, received his Mexican land grant of one and one-fourth leagues on July 15, 1824. Stephen F. Austin and the Baron de Bastrop signed it. His land stretched for about one and a half miles along the north or east bank of the Brazos River and stretched about five miles north. The present-day town of Simonton in Fort Bend County is situated on the old Noel F. Roberts League.

Roberts first married Highley Carter on March 10, 1808, in Clarke County, Georgia. They had three sons: John Hardin, William Taylor, and Josiah. John Hardin and his mother both died in 1817. William and Josiah went to Texas with their father.

Roberts next married Morning Harper in Lawrence County, Mississippi, on November 19, 1820. There were probably a son and a daughter born to this marriage as the 1826 census to Austin's Colony lists Noel F. as widower age forty to fifty, farmer and stockraiser. He had four slaves, one son under seven years of age, two sons between seven and sixteen, and one daughter under seven. If Morning Harper came to Texas, she died before 1826.

He next married Harriet Pryor by marriage bond on July 26, 1826. Harriet was the oldest child of William Pryor, another of the Old Three Hundred families. To this marriage were born Elisha, Hirma, John, Mary, and Thomas Roberts.

Noel's son William married Elizabeth "Betsy" Pryor, William Pryor's youngest daughter. William and Josiah fought in the Texas Revolution. William was in the Battle of San Jacinto. He and Betsy walked the battlefield the next day with Betsy carrying her first-born son.

Noel died in the fall of 1843, leaving a large estate.

Source:
James Edgar Roberts #488

ROBERT SCOBEY

Robert Scobey was born circa 1802 in Tennessee, the son of Robert Scobey and Lucy Debow. He married Mary L. Fulshear, daughter of Churchill Fulshear and Betsy Summer Fulshear, September 5, 1821, in Tennessee.

Young Scobey and his wife traveled with his father-in-law's family to Texas in the fall of 1823 and had their first child, Andrew Wilkinson Scobey, in Arkansas on August 12, 1823. They made it to Texas in time to join Stephen F. Austin's Old Three Hundred, receiving a *sitio* of land in present-day Wharton County, August 3, 1824.

By the 1826 Census, he and his wife had another son, Matthew, born January 1, 1826. After they had met their obligations on their land grant in Wharton County, they sold it and moved to Brazoria County, between West Columbia and Angleton.

Scobey opened a tavern between San Felipe and Harrisburg in January 1832. He drove a wagon loaded with rifles and ammunition to Goliad and contributed supplies to the Texas Army during the Texas Revolution.

Mary L. Fulshear Scobey died October 7, 1837, in Brazoria County. In 1846 Robert Scobey was administrator to the estate of Elisha M. Adcock in Harris County. In 1852 he married Rebecca Adcock. His will was dated August 16, 1855, and probated October 30, 1855 in Brazoria County, leaving his estate to his children: Andrew Wilkinson, married Rebecca Little on January 23, 1839; Matthew; Elizabeth J., born January 2, 1828, married (a) to Stephen Jackson Justice in 1842, and (b) to Abraham H. Kipp on November 2, 1857; Sytha Douglas, born 1830, married (a) to F. M. Jackson in 1845 and (b) to Albert Brown Sweden; Mary Jane, born August 6, 1832, married (a) to Harvey N. Little and (b) to Harry Newton.

Sources:
Cheryl B. (Sissie) Kipp #3
John Emmette (Dick) Kipp #113

JAMES SCOTT

Born circa 1780 in Berkeley County, Virginia, to Revolutionary War veteran George Scott and Angeletta (Craighill) Scott, James Scott found new battles to fight in Texas.

In 1822 James and his brother William arrived at Austin's Colony, where James received a league of land on the San Bernard River in present-day Fort Bend County and William received two leagues and a *labor* in present-day Harris County. James later left the colony for a period of years, marrying a widow, Jane (Malgrave) McClean in 1827 in Dubois County, Indiana. (He was previously married to Mary Lafever in Frederick County, Virginia.) James and Jane had three children: William Craighill, George Russell, and James William.

James returned to Texas in 1834. Sometime before February 1836, the family relocated from the San Bernard to Cedar Bayou (near present-day Baytown in Harris County). He died in 1845 and his widow in 1873. Records indicate James was a Mason.

Records also show that he volunteered for a three-month hitch with the Texas Army after the Battle of Gonzales in October 1835. James probably participated in the "Grass Fight" and other early skirmishes. He was awarded bounty land for taking part in the Siege of Bexar, after which he doubtless decided the war was over and went home to plant crops. William also took part in the action at Bexar.

Source:
Esther Smith Halbert #117

DANIEL SHIPMAN

Daniel Shipman, born in Kentucky on February 20, 1801, was the son of Moses Shipman of North Carolina and Mary Robinson, daughter of John Robinson of South Carolina.

In *Frontier Life*, Shipman wrote: "The 9th of March 1822 we crossed over Red River into Texas; and have lived in Texas ever since. It was a new country, new acquaintances, and new things generally."

He and his family settled on Mill Creek near San Felipe in March 1823.

In 1825 the settlers in the coastal region had trouble with the Karankawas, and Colonel Austin asked for fifty volunteers to drive the Indians out of the area. Daniel was one of the fifty volunteers. The group trailed the Indians to the Guadalupe River before a peace agreement was arranged.

On May 21, 1827, Daniel and his partner, Charles L. Nidever, received title to a league of land in present Brazoria County. They formed one of Austin's Old Three Hundred families.

On September 23, 1828, Daniel married Margaretta Kelley, the daughter of John and Sarah Kelley, also of Austin's Old Three Hundred. Daniel and Margaretta had a daughter, Mary Jane, in 1829, and their son, John Kelley, was born October 30, 1831. After the death of his first wife, Margaretta, Daniel married Eliza Hancock, daughter of Thomas Hancock. They had one son, Edward Moses, born January 18, 1840. They lived near Brenham in Washington County and also maintained a ranch in Goliad County. Eliza died on September 11, 1858.

Shipman served Texas well. Under the command of Francis W. Johnson in 1832, he joined the company that attacked Juan Davis Bradburn at Anahuac. When General Cos invaded Texas to establish a stronghold in San Antonio, and Austin issued a call to arms, Daniel, with his brother Moses and his brother-in-law John Owens, enlisted in the Texas Volunteer Army and marched to Bexar. Daniel participated in the fight that caused Cos to surrender and leave Texas.

In the fall of 1870 Daniel wrote a series of articles about his experiences in Texas in the *Houston Telegraph,* and in 1879, at the age of seventy-eight, he published *Frontier Life,* his reminiscences of his early life and days in Texas.

Daniel Shipman died March 4, 1881, in Goliad County at the age of seventy-nine. He is buried beside his second wife in a cemetery near Weesatche. On June 15, 1938, Daniel and Eliza were reinterred in the State Cemetery in Austin.

Source:
Helen Shipman Cunningham #192

MOSES SHIPMAN

Moses Shipman was born about 1775 in North Carolina. On January 19, 1798, Moses married Mary Robinson of South Carolina, and they became parents of ten children, nine of whom lived to adulthood.

The Shipman family left South Carolina in 1814, moving to Tennessee, Illinois, and Missouri. In October of 1821 the family began their journey to Texas.

The trip was slow and tedious since the roads were bad, with many deep gullies and muddy creeks to cross. In December, while traveling through Arkansas, Mary gave birth to their youngest child, Lucinda. Before they reached Texas they sold or gave away everything they could not carry and made the final trip on horseback, crossing the Red River at Jonesborough on March 9, 1822. After receiving a favorable report on Stephen F. Austin's colony, the family moved to the Brazos River, and settled near San Felipe in the fork of Mill Creek and the Brazos River.

Moses Shipman received a league of land in present-day Fort Bend County and a *labor* of land in present Austin County on July 19, 1824.

While the family was living on Mill Creek in 1825, Joseph Bays, a Baptist minister and a friend from Missouri, came to visit. Although contrary to Mexican law under which they were living, the Reverend Bays was allowed to hold a service in the Shipman home. Probably this was the first Baptist sermon preached west of the Brazos River.

In 1825 the Shipmans moved to their league on Oyster Creek, southeast of the present town of Richmond. They built a house which had two rooms with wooden floors, a lean-to, and a rain barrel. Some of the Shipmans lived on this league for over fifty years.

The Shipmans were involved in events leading to the Texas Revolution. Moses Shipman was the president of the election at the home of John Owens to choose delegates to the Convention of 1836 at Washington-on-the-Brazos.

Moses Shipman died in Fort Bend County in late 1836. His wife, Mary, remained on the league until her death.

Source:
Helen Shipman Cunningham #192

Aylett C. Buckner was a red-haired, 6'6, 250-pound giant of a man. He came to Texas the first time in 1812 and built a house on the Colorado River before Austin arrived. In the beginning, Buckner and Austin had several disagreements but became good friends.

Known for his rough manner and incredible strength, Buckner has been the subject of many stories. It was said that he could kill a yearling with one blow of his fist. He gained a reputation as a great hunter, choosing to use, instead of guns, his bare fist or a tomahawk to get wild game. A Karankawa said he saw Buckner stop a wildcat in midair with one swing.

Buckner was later ranked by *Harper's Magazine* as the equal of Paul Bunyan.

CAPT. BARTLETT SAMUEL SIMS

Capt. Bartlett Samuel Sims was born in 1773, in Tennessee. In 1824, two years after coming to Texas, he married Sarah Curtis, the daughter of James Curtis, in Burleson County. They had three sons: James Curtis, William Anderson, Thomas McKinney; and six daughters: Mary E., Margaret A., Eugenia Missouria, Emily V., Josephine, and Sarah.

In October 1824, Stephen Austin contracted with Captain Sims to start the northern part of the colony. At this time, Captain Sims was living in a two-room dirt-floor cabin, south of the Old Spanish Road on the Brazos River. He surveyed roads, *labors,* and leagues of land, most of which are in now Burleson and Washington counties.

Bartlett Sims was treasurer for Mina (Bastrop) County for a number of years, and county surveyor from 1836 to 1840. He was a Christian gentleman, very generous, with the unusual ability to lead. His devotion to the cause of freedom was outstanding. He is said to be one of the two founders of the famous Texas Rangers.

In 1846, Bartlett Sims started on a surveying expedition to the Pedernales River, with his nephew, William Sims, and chain-carriers Clark and Grant. They were attacked by a party of Indians and all were killed, except Captain Sims, who managed to escape.

Bartlett Sims died circa 1863 at Rice's Crossing. Sarah Curtis Sims died in 1876. Both were buried in a cemetery on a cliff on the old Brushy Creek in Williamson County. The cemetery was washed away during floods in the 1900s.

Source:
Corine Crossland Thomas #21

PHILLIP SINGLETON

Phillip Singleton was married to Susanna Walker on June 14, 1815, in Wayne County, Kentucky.

On August 16, 1824, he was granted land from Stephen F. Austin. Witnessing the transaction were David McCormick and Samuel M. Williams. The land was located on the south and north sides of Yegua Creek, where it empties into the Brazos River. By 1828-29, the family moved to the San Jacinto-Lynchburg area. Phillip had possession of 171+ acres of land across Buffalo Bayou, opposite the San Jacinto Battlegrounds. There he built a log house and later covered it with sawmill planks and added glass windows. According to *Burke's Almanac*, it was the first house to have such amenities. It was later sold to Lorenzo de Zavala. This house was used as a hospital for the Texian troops during the Battle of San Jacinto.

The 1826 census shows Phillip as a farmer/stockraiser between forty and fifty years of age; Susana in the same age bracket; two male children between seven and sixteen; two male children between sixteen and twenty-five; one female under seven; and one female between seven and sixteen.

Phillip Singleton spent the last years of his life on the banks of the San Jacinto River. The cause of his death and his burial place are unknown. It is said that he went hunting and never returned. On the legal documents concerning the estate, Spyars, James W., and Phillip Singleton were named as sons.

Many of his descendants have remained in the area of his home.

Source:
Shirley Jean Hanagriff Stedman #53

CHRISTIAN SMITH

Christian Smith was born in 1774 in Stokes County, North Carolina. His father was possibly Christian Schmidt, a German immigrant. He was married to Rachel Poffard or Paffard, who was born in North Carolina in 1774.

Christian Smith moved to Kentucky sometime between 1803 and 1809 and was in Texas by July 19, 1824, when he received a *sitio* of land in the present area of Harris and Chambers counties. He was residing in the San Jacinto District in November of 1824, when he signed a petition for appointment of a surveyor in the area. He was one of twenty-three men who were recruited to spend three months in Galveston in case Santa Anna sent a fleet of ships there.

In the Atascosito District census of July 31, 1826, Christian Smith was listed as a carpenter aged over fifty, with a wife, four sons, and a daughter.

Christian Smith's granddaughter Elizabeth married Edward Este, who went on the Mier Expedition and was one of the unfortunate ones who drew a black bean and was shot.

Christian Smith died in 1839, possibly in Tennessee, where his son Joseph lived. His estate was probated in Harrisburg. His wife, Rachel, died in 1845 in Cedar Bayou.

Their children were born in North Carolina: John, circa 1798, Joseph, circa 1800, Elizabeth, 1803, and Eleanor, 1809.

Source:
Charles "Douglas" McBee, Jr. #176

CORNELIUS SMITH

Cornelius Smith was born on December 23, 1783, in Rowan County, North Carolina. He was the son of Thomas B. and Molly Smith. His marriage on January 21, 1808, to Elizabeth Roberts was in Pulaski County, Kentucky. Twelve children were born to them: Margaret Elizabeth, John B., William Robert, Mary (Polly), Lucriata, Cornelius, Rachel, Gaines, C. Henry, Wesley Lee, James, and Elizabeth.

Cornelius was among the Old Three Hundred and appears on the first census of Texas in 1826 with his family. He received grant No. 191 on August 10, 1824.

Cornelius Smith died on October 10, 1837, according to the Cornelius Smith Bible. In the 1850 census, his wife Betsy is shown in Brazoria County as head of a household. She died about 1859.

The grave of Cornelius has not been found but is believed to be in Brazoria County. Some of his children immigrated to the West Fork of Plum Creek in Caldwell County to make their home. A chapter of the Daughters of the Republic of Texas in Caldwell County has been named in his honor because so many of his descendants live there today.

Source:
Maxine Moses Henderson #138

ADAM STAFFORD

Adam Stafford, the son of William and Martha (Donnell) Stafford, was born February 5, 1806, in North Carolina. In 1824 he journeyed from Tennessee to join his father in Austin's Colony. On August 24, 1824, despite having no wife or partner, he received a *labor* of land located in present Waller County. He farmed in Fort Bend County.

Handicapped at the time of the Texas Revolution, Adam Stafford saw no action. He did, however, furnish supplies to the Texas Army. During the Runaway Scrape, he sent his servants to accompany his family and neighbors while he took the cattle on a different road to ford the San Jacinto River.

Adam married Maria Elizabeth Hankins in 1842 in Richmond. Their children were Sarah, Martha, Margaret (Bettie), Mary Ella, and William Hankins. Only Martha and Bettie would survive their long-lived father. In 1846, reportedly wanting to live in a larger town, the family moved to Victoria, where Adam Stafford became a land owner and horse breeder of note. His wife died there on November 8, 1855. Adam lived on until November 21, 1880.

Adam Stafford's obituary reads, in part: "The deceased was eccentric in disposition, but warm hearted and kind withal. To his friends he was the truest of friends—his enemies he had none. He attained a ripe old age, respected most by those who knew him best."

Source:
Wincie Chenault Campbell #215

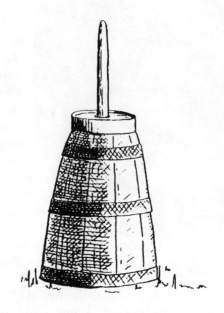

WILLIAM STAFFORD

According to a petition authored and signed by his friends not long before he died, William Stafford was an "orderly, peaceable, honest, enterprising, patriotic and philanthropic citizen" of the Republic of Texas.

Research indicates that Stafford was born about 1780 in North Carolina. There he married Martha Donnell and they had four children: Adam (also an original grantee), Sarah, Harvey, and Mary. After his wife's death he married Martha Cartwright on May 28, 1818, in Wilson County, Tennessee. Their children were Martha, William Joseph, Jr., Susan, and John Thomas.

Two years after his arrival in San Felipe, Stafford on August 16, 1824, was granted one and a half leagues on Oyster Creek in present Fort Bend County and a *labor* in present Waller County. He established his plantation on the creek near Stafford Lake, where he built a cane mill and reportedly had the first horse-powered cotton gin in the colony. He has also been credited with introducing sugar cane to the area. A second Stafford home on the nearby prairie (Stafford's Point) sat on the future site of his namesake city.

In 1835 Stafford slayed a man named Moore which caused him to flee the country. In his absence, and after his family abandoned their home in the face of the invading Mexican army in April of 1836, Santa Anna put the plantation buildings to the torch. Stafford returned home in 1838 following the success of his friends' petition to secure an executive clemency for the slaying.

Stafford died in 1840.

Source:
Wincie Chenault Campbell #215

JESSE THOMPSON

Jesse Thompson was born in Georgia around 1776. Jesse was a big man with blue eyes and light colored hair. He married Mary Denley in Alabama, where most of their nine children were born. Their children were: Hiram M., James M., John D., Jesse M., Mary, Grace Elizabeth, Eliza Jane, Henry C., and Lavinia.

In 1823 Jesse and his family moved to Austin's Colony. He located his league in Brazoria County, which was granted to him on August 7, 1824, by the Mexican government. Austin's 1826 census listed Jesse Thompson as a farmer and stockraiser. His household included his wife, four sons, four daughters, two servants, and fifteen slaves.

In about 1828 Jesse came to the Fort Settlement and contracted for one-fourth of the Knight & White league on the east side of the Brazos River. This became the Thompson plantation. He also bought from Knight & White's agent the *labor* across the river from the plantation. He put in a ferry crossing there in the early 1830s.

Thompson's Ferry holds a special place in history. According to the diary of Colonel Almonte of the Mexican army, on April 11, 1836, there was firing across the river between General Santa Anna's and Capt. Wyly Martin's men at Thompson's Crossing. This confrontation is known as the "Battle at Thompson's Crossing." On April 14 the ferry was seized by a detachment of Santa Anna's army and used to cross the Brazos in pursuit of Gen. Sam Houston. Fort Bend County records show that the ferry was operated by the Thompson family until 1866.

Jesse Thompson was killed in 1834. Mary died May 2, 1856.

Descendants of Jesse Thompson reportedly lived on the farm as late as 1939. In 1936 the Texas Centennial Commission erected a monument near the site of the ferry on this same property.

Source:
Stephen H. Lubojacky #67

ELIZABETH TUMLINSON

Elizabeth Tumlinson, her husband John Jackson, Sr., three daughters and three of their sons, originally from North Carolina, arrived at Austin's Colony in 1821.

John Jackson Tumlinson was appointed the first *alcalde* from their district. He was credited with forming a group of men who became the forerunners of the Texas Rangers. He was also the first man from that organization to lose his life in the line of duty. He was killed by Wacos as he was on his way to San Antonio for supplies and ammunition. His body was never found.

Jackson's widow was given a land grant of a league and a *labor* August 16, 1824, on the south bank of the Colorado River, where the town of Columbus is now located. As she was led by the hand and told how by the virtue of the land commissioners and the Mexican government she now possessed this land for herself, her heirs and successors, she had her dream of a permanent home. But she never imagined her family would have to pay such a high price as John's life. She fought back tears as she followed the ritual requirements and shouted aloud, pulled herbs, threw stones, set stakes, and performed the necessary ceremonies. When it was over, Elizabeth stood tall. She had her children and there was work to do.

Elizabeth died in Colorado County in 1833.

Source:
Nadine Frances Dees Hays #74

JAMES WALKER, SR.

James Walker was born in 1762. He married Catherine Miller on September 9, 1783. They had a total of fifteen children: Catherine, Sally, Lucretia, James, John, William, Elizabeth, Sanders, Charles, Andrew, Susanna, Gideon, Lucinda, Thomas, and one died young.

In 1790 James and his family (which consisted of the wife and three children at that time) left Virginia and settled in Wayne County, Kentucky. The others were apparently born there.

Soon after their arrival in Kentucky, rumors were spreading about greater and better land in Texas, so they began to plan on moving again.

On July 21, 1824, after their trek to Texas, they joined Stephen F. Austin's colonists. Walker's land grant was in Washington County.

After receiving word in 1835 of the impending war with Mexico, James signed up and fought for independence from Mexico.

James Walker died in 1837. His estate was administered by his son Gideon.

Source:
Marilyn R. Thacker #271

AMY COMSTOCK WHITE

Amy White was born Amelia Comstock on March 10, 1775, in Rhode Island, the daughter of William Comstock and Rachel Aldrich. She was married in St. Martinville, Louisiana, on January 31, 1791, to William White, the son of John White and Sarah Gambill of Virginia. William White was born in North Carolina in 1766 and died on the Vermilion River in 1821 at his land grant in present Vermilion Parish. He and Amy raised a family of ten children.

The depressed economic conditions of the 1820s made many Louisiana families look west to Texas, where the land was being opened up to immigrants by the new Republic of Mexico. In 1824 Amy and seven of her children became a part of Austin's first contract for families to settle in Texas. Daughter Rachel had married and stayed behind, as did son Jesse White, who took care of family business before coming to Texas in 1829. Daughter Mary, who was married to William Whitlock, and son Reuben White were also among the Old Three Hundred.

Amy White and her children, as well as friends from Louisiana, selected grants along the San Jacinto River, and formed the White Settlement above the present-day town of Highlands. They were listed in the Atascosito Census of 1826.

In about 1827, Amy married a new arrival from Ireland named William Swail. After the death of her second husband in the 1830s, Amy lived for a while with her daughter Mary Whitlock in Liberty County. She then lived with her son William White, Jr., at the White Settlement. The 1850 census shows her in his household. She died in 1853.

Her sons William and Jesse, and sons-in-law, grandson, and other eligible men in the family participated in the Battle of San Jacinto and other actions of the Texas Revolution.

Source:
Gifford White #40

89

WILLIAM WHITLOCK

William Whitlock was born in 1784 in Caswell County, North Carolina. He was the son of Robert and Aggy (Stringer) Whitlock. The family appeared in Ninety-Six District of South Carolina for the 1790 and 1800 census.

As a young man William moved to Louisiana, where on February 16, 1813, he married Mary White, daughter of William and Amy Comstock White. Their marriage is recorded in St. Martin's Church, St. Martinville, Louisiana.

William and Mary Whitlock and their children joined the extended family of the widowed Amy White to move to Texas in 1824 to enter the first colony of Stephen F. Austin. On August 13, 1824, William Whitlock made his petition for land to Baron de Bastrop and became one of Austin's Old Three Hundred. He was granted a league on the east bank of the San Jacinto River near the grants of the other Amy White family members.

William and Mary Whitlock had three sons: Robert, Bernard, and Henry; and four daughters: Elizabeth, Amanda, Rachel, and Martha. Son Robert and husbands of the married daughters joined the Texian forces at the Battle of San Jacinto and otherwise aided in the revolution against Mexico.

William Whitlock and family were in the Atascosito Census of 1826, where he appeared as a farmer and stockraiser. Three of his children were born in Texas. In March 1835 he died in Liberty County, Texas.

Source:
Mary S. Maxfield #46

THOMAS WILLIAMS

Thomas Williams was born between 1771 and 1773 in Kentucky. He married Nancy Johnson (Gilleland), widow of William Gilleland, on September 15, 1802, in Davidson County, Tennessee. Nancy was born circa 1773-1775 in Kentucky.

By 1807 the Thomas Williams family was living in Arkansas Territory. The children born there to them were Benjamin, who died on the way to Texas; Thomas Johnson, born November 7, 1807, and who died October 5, 1889, in Matagorda County, Texas; Nancy, born 1809; and Mary Diane, born 1811 and who died in Texas.

In 1820 the family left Arkansas for Texas bringing pack horses, cattle, and hogs. Caleb Bostic and John Ingram traveled with them. In January 1821 the travelers crossed the Colorado River and settled about eight miles above present-day Columbus.

In June of 1823, Williams, Bostic, Thomas Jamison, and Moses Morrison cut a path down to Bay Prairie and then to Cedar Lake in Matagorda County, where the Williams family relocated. The Karankawas were an ever-present threat to the colonists; members of a neighboring family were killed.

On July 4, 1824 or 1825, Thomas Williams died from exposure at fifty-three years of age. Nancy was left with three children to rear in a wild new land. On August 16, 1824, Stephen F. Austin granted a league of land to the name of Thomas Williams. In 1833 Nancy divided this land among her children. She died in Travis County about 1854.

Source:
Betty Jo Ray Rusk #532

ZADOCK WOODS

Zadock Woods, son of Jonathan, Jr., and Keziah Keith Woods, was born September 18, 1773, in Brookfield, Massachusetts.

In Woodstock, Vermont, in 1796, Woods met Minerva Cottle, daughter of Joseph Cottle. They were married in 1797. The children and spouses were as follows: Minerva, 1798-1897 married William Harrell 1796-1891; Ardelia, 1804, lived seven months; Norman, 1805-1857, married Jane Boyd Wells, 1809-1866; Montraville, 1806-1857, married Isabella Gonzales; Leander,1809-1832; and Henry Gonzalvo, 1816-1867, married Jane Boyd Wells.

The grant on which Woods finally settled was a few miles above LaGrange in the Colorado River Valley—Indian country. A Texas Centennial historical marker has been placed on the site of the Woods Fort, which was used by colonists as protection against Indian attacks. It stands 1.5 miles west of West Point on Texas Highway 71.

In September 1842 Captain Dawson called for volunteers to face General Woll in San Antonio. The Woods boys, Norman and Gonzalvo, immediately hid their father's horse and made an emphatic declaration that the old man was not to undertake the ride to San Antonio. Zadock declared he would ride with them or he would walk without them. Said he, "I fought with Andrew Jackson at New Orleans, and with old Sam Houston at San Jacinto, and I just give the enemy one more crack at old Zadock." There were five Woods men in this group: Zadock, Norman, Gonzalvo, and Zadock's grandsons, John Wesley Pendleton and seventeen-year-old Milvern Harrell.

The Battle of San Antonio was fierce. Norman was wounded and Zadock was killed when he went to his aid. In 1848 their remains were disinterred and entombed in the old Rock Tomb on Monument Hill overlooking the wide sweep of the Colorado River Valley.

Zadock Woods, on his sixty-ninth birthday, died for what he believed in—liberty and family. Minerva Cottle Woods had died in 1839. She is buried in the Woods Cemetery at Woods Prairie in Fayette County.

Source:
Mrs. Lewis Asbal Parr #32

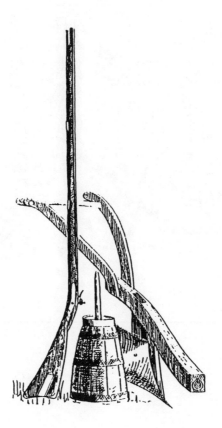

REFERENCES

Martin Allen

References:
Allen, Miles Newton. Wallis, Texas. Personal interview.
Barker, Eugene C. *The Life of Stephen F. Austin.* Austin, Texas: The University of Texas Press, 1949.
Davis, Robert E., editor. *Diary of William Barret Travis.* Waco, Texas: Texian Press, 1966.
Dilue W. Harris, and B. M. Hulse. *History of Claiborne Parish.*
Duval, John C. *Early Times in Texas.* Austin, Texas: Steck Co., 1935.
Erickson, Joe E. *Judges of the Republic of Texas.* Dallas, Texas: Taylor Publishing Co., 1980.
Grisham, Noel. *Crossroads at San Felipe.* Burnet, Texas: Eakin Press, 1980.
Hollon, W. Eugene, and Ruth L. Butler. *William Bollaert's Texas.* Norman, Oklahoma: University of Oklahoma Press, 1956.
Schwartz, Fred, and Robert H. Thonhoff. *Forgotten Battlefield.* Austin, Texas: Eakin Press, 1985.
Tracy, Milton Cook, and Richard Havelock-Bailie. *The Colonizer.* El Paso, Texas: Guynes Printing Co., 1941.

Charles G. Alsbury

References:
Lewis, W. S. "Adventures of the *Lively* Immigrants." *Quarterly of the Texas State Historical Association,* vol. 3 (1899), nos. 1 and 2.
Renner, Helen Ruth. *The Alsbury Gleanings From the Midwest,* p. 231.
Texas General Land Office. Austin's "Old 300." Land grant #177.

DR. HORACE ARLINGTON ALSBURY

References:
"The San Jacinto Campaign." *Texas Historical Association Quarterly*, vol. 4 (1900-01), pp. 339-340.
Daughters of the Republic of Texas. *Muster Rolls of the Texas Revolution*. Austin, Texas: DRT, 1986, p. 43.
Dixon, S. H., and L. W. Kemp. *The Heroes of San Jacinto*. Houston, Texas: The Anson Jones Press, 1932, p. 308.
Groneman, Bill. *Alamo Defenders*. Austin, Texas: Eakin Press, 1990, p. 5.
―――. *Roll Call at the Alamo*, p. 83.
Letter of Y. P. Alsbury of October 1, 1859. Center for American History, The Unviersity of Texas, Austin, Texas.
Roll of Captain Thomas Alsbury's Company, First Regiment Kentucky Mounted Militia. Soldiers of the War of 1812, Kentucky Archives.
Spurlin, Charles D. *Texas Veterans in the Mexican War*. Austin, Texas: Eakin Press, 1998.
Texas Almanac 1861, pp. 55-58.
Texas as Province and Republic. Reel 1, Texas Imprints nos. 1-120.
Texas General Land Office. Austin's "Old 300." Land grants #42 and #177.
Texas State Archives. San Jacinto List. Major General Sam Houston's Army Roster, p. 30.
―――. Petition for pension for Mrs. Juana Alsbury.

CAPT. THOMAS ALSBURY

References:
"Hanson Alsbury to S. F. Austin, June 1, 1827." Austin Papers. Center for American History, The University of Texas at Austin.
"Juana Navarro Alsbury, September 18, 1870." Pension Applications. Texas State Archives.
Brazoria Board of Land Commissioners. Land Certificate, March 15, 1832.
Daughters of the Republic of Texas. "York's Company," in *Muster Rolls of Texas Revolution*. Austin, Texas: DRT, Inc., 1986.
Killebrew, J. T. *Court Order Book, Christian County, Kentucky*.
―――. *Deed Book, Christian County, Kentucky*.
Perrin, W. H. *County of Christian, Kentucky*.
Point Pleasant Battle Commission, Charleston, West Virginia.
Renner, Helen Ruth. *Alsbury Gleanings from the Midwest*.
Roll of Captain Thomas Alsbury's Company, First Regiment Kentucky Mounted Militia. Soldiers of the War of 1812, Kentucky Archives.
Spurlin, Charles. *Texas Veterans in the Mexican War*. Austin: Eakin Press, 1998.
Stephen F. Austin's letter to Alsbury dated May 4, 1824. Center for American History, The University of Texas, Austin.
Texas General Land Office. Austin's "Old 300." Land grant #42.
Texas State Archives. San Jacinto List.

96

WILLIAM ANDREWS

References:
General Land Office, Austin, Texas. *Abstract of Original Titles of Record.*
Hebert, Rev. Donald J. *Southwest Louisiana Records*, vol. 2. Eunice, Louisiana: The author, 1974.
Moore, Bill. *Bastrop County 1691-1900.* Wichita Falls, Texas: Nortex Press, 1977.
Resolution of the House of Representatives, May 24, 1838.
U. S. Census. 1810. St. Landry Parish, Louisiana.
Wharton, Clarence R. *History of Fort Bend County.* Houston: Anson Jones Press, 1939.

JAMES BRITTON BAILEY

References:
Gholson, Josephine Polley. *Bailey's Light.* San Antonio: Naylor, 1950, pp. 33-82.
Wharton, Clarence R. *History of Fort Bend County.* Houston: Anson Jones Press, 1939, p. 50.

WILLIAM BARRET (BARRETT)

References:
Bible data furnished by Edgar Barrett, who resides on the Thomas William Barrett farm between Nixon and Stockdale where Thomas Wiliam Barrett's body is buried.
Brazoria County, Texas. Barrett et al. Vol. G, File 177.
———. Deed Book, Vol. A, p. 423.
———. Vol. A, 1829-1852, p. 30, #4.
———. Vol. A, p. 200, #134.
Texas General Land Office. "Austin Colony," Vol. II, pp. 3-4, Vol. VIII, pp. 685-688.
Texas State Archives, Austin, Texas. Discharge papers of William Barrett.
Wilson County (Texas) Courthouse. File 182.

BENJAMIN BEASON

References:
Johnson, Frank W., and E. C. Barker. *The History of Texas and Texans.* Chicago: American Historical Society, 1914.
Williams, Amelia, and E. C. Barker, editors. *The Writings of Sam Houston.* Austin: The University of Texas Press, 1938.

ISAAC BEST

References:
Best, Isaac. File. Waller County Historical Museum.
Bryan, William S., and Robert Rose. *A History of the Pioneer Families of Missouri.* Reprint. Baltimore: 1984.
Mouser, Lafrona Foshee. *A Genealogy of the Mouser Ancestry Including the Best and Other Families.* Oklahoma City: 1978.
Mullins, Marion Day. *The First Census of Texas, 1829-1836.* Washington, D.C.: National Genealogical Society, 1976.
Shuman, Mrs. Sam. *A History of Waller County, Texas.*
Taylor, Virginia H. *The Spanish Archives of the General Land Office of Texas.* Austin: 1955.

EDWARD R. BRADLEY

References:
Bradley/Dodson Family Bible.
French Tipton Papers. Eastern Kentucky University, Richmond, Kentucky.
Kentucky Tax Rolls, 1788.
Letter from Archeleus B. Dodson to Mrs. Looscan, 1892.
Lincoln County, Kentucky. Marriage Records, 1787.
Plat of Austin's Old Three Hundred Land Grants.
Winn, George. Will probated in Clark County, Kentucky, 1803.

CHARLES C. BREEN

References:
U.S. Census 1850. Williamson County, Texas. National Archives Microfilm M432, Roll 916.
U.S. Census 1860. Williamson County, Texas. National Archives Microfilm M653, Roll 1308.
White, Gifford. *1840 Citizens of Texas.* Vol. 2, Tax Rolls. Austin: 1984.

WILLIAM B. BRIDGES

References:
Circuit Court Records of Clark County, Arkansas. Deposition #3615, P. B. Lyons et al. vs. William S. Lyons et al., Book B, p. 81.
Clerk of the Court's Office, LaGrange, Fayette County, Texas, Vol. C, p. 354.
Ericson, Joe E. *Judges of the Republic of Texas 1836-1846.* Dallas: Taylor Publishing Co., 1980.

Texas General Land Office. "Clerk's Reports" file.
Texas General Land Office. Mexican Colonial Grant, Vol. I, p. 194.
Texas State Archives. Discharge papers, William B. Bridges. File #7433.
White, Gifford. *1840 Citizens of Texas*. Vol. III. Austin: 1988.

DAVID BRIGHT

References:
Augusta County, Virginia, Court Records. Marriages Book I.
First Census of Texas. Residents of the Colorado District, March 4, 1823.
Fort Bend County, Texas. Court Records.
Hawley Cemetery Association. *Deming's Bridge Cemetery-Hawley Cemetery-Tres Palacios Baptist Church*, 1977, p. 6.
Matagorda County Probate Record filed March 2, 1842.
Matagorda County Probate Record, Book A, filed September 14, 1837.
"Notes and Fragments." *Southwestern Historical Quarterly*, XXVI (1922-1923).
Texas General Land Office. Spanish Land Grants.
U.S. Census, Matagorda County, Texas. 1850. National Archives Microfilm M432, Roll 912.
U.S. Census, Matagorda County, Texas. 1860. National Archives Microfilm M653, Roll 1300.
U.S. Census, Matagorda County, Texas. 1870. National Archives Microfilm M593, Roll 1597.
Wharton, Clarence R. *History of Fort Bend County*. Houston: Anson Jones Press, 1939.

CAPT. JESSE BURNAM

References:
"Reminiscences of Captain Jesse Burnam." *Quarterly of the Texas State Historical Association*, vol. V (1901-1902).
Colorado County Historical Survey Committee. *Early Settlers and Bits of History of Columbus and Colorado County, 1821-1845*.
Shuffler, R. Henderson. "Winedale Inn, at Early Texas' Cultural Crossroad." *Texas Quarterly* (Summer 1965), vol. VIII: no. 2, pp. 132-134.
Sinks, Julia Lee. *Chronicles of Fayette*.
Weyand, Leonie Rummel, and Houston Wade. *An Early History of Fayette County*. LaGrange, Texas: LaGrange Journal, 1936, pp. 85-92.
Williams, Marjorie L., editor. *Fayette County: Past & Present*, LaGrange, Texas: The author, 1976, pp. 328-329.

MICAJAH BYRD

References:
The *Galveston News,* November 11, 1884, quoting the *Navasota Tabloid.*
Hatch, Aldon. *The Byrds of Virginia.* 1969.
Pollard, Charleen Plumly. "Civil War letters of George W. Allen." *Southwestern Historical Quarterly,* vol. LXXXIII, no. 1 (July 1979).
Quarterly of the Texas State Historical Association, vol. VI, pp. 236-237.
Star of the Republic, vol. XLII, no. 2.
Texas Census of 1823 and 1826.
Thrall, Homer S. *Pictorial History of Texas.*

SYLVANUS CASTLEMAN

References:
Davidson County [Tennessee] Marriage Book I, January 2, 1789-December 13, 1837.
Davidson County [Tennessee] Minutes, Book 1809-1812, p. 826.
Gulick, Charles Adams, Jr., editor. *Papers of Mirabeau B. Lamar.* Vol. IV. Austin: Von Boeckmann-Jones, 1920.
Weyand, Leonie R., and Houston Wade. *History of Fayette County.* LaGrange, Texas: LaGrange Journal, 1936.
Williams, Annie Lee. *History of Wharton County 1846-1961.* Austin: Von Boeckmann-Jones, 1964.
Winkler, Ernest W. *Manuscript Letters & Documents of Early Texians, 1821-1845.* Austin: The Steck Co., 1937.

JOHN CRIER

References:
Church Archives of St. Augustine Parish, Florida. Historical Records Survey. Entry 383.
Colorado County, Texas. Marriage Records. Vol. B, p. 131.
Colorado County, Texas. Probate Court. Case #307, 11-14-1856.
Fayette County, Texas. County Clerk Records, vol. J, p. 214, #3144.
General Land Office, Austin, Texas. Spanish Archives.
Weyand, Leonie R., and Houston Wade. *Early History of Fayette County.* LaGrange, Texas: LaGrange Journal, 1936.
Salley, A. S. *History of Orangeburg County, S.C., 1704-1782.* Baltimore: Genealogical Publishing Co., 1978.
Texas State Library, Austin, Texas. Manuscript notes of Louis W. Kemp.
Veteran's Administration, Washington, D.C. Pension Claim S31635.
Williams, Villamae. *Stephen F. Austin's Register of Families.* St. Louis, Missouri: Ingmire Publications, 1984.

REBEKAH CUMINGS

References:
Austin County Colonial Archives, Bellville, Texas. Book II, pp. 306-311.
Austin County Wills. File Drawer 8, Packet 28.
Haskew, Corrie Pattison. *Historical Records of Austin and Waller Counties*. Houston: 1969.
Henderson County, Kentucky. Deed Book E, p. 282.
Jackson, Evelyn, and William Talley. *Eastern Kentucky References*. Owensboro, Kentucky, 1980, p. 109.
Lewis County, Kentucky. Tax List. 1807.
Private correspondence, May Biggs to Mrs. B. L. Smythe and Mrs. J. R. Sanders, October 31, 1951.
Texas General Land Office, Austin, Texas. Spanish Archives. Title to Rebekah Cummings *[sic]*.

JAMES (JACK) CUMMINS

References:
Colorado County Historical Commission. *Colorado County Chronicles*. Austin: Nortex Press, 1986, vol. I, p. 43.
Lucas, Silas Emmett, Jr., editor. *Davidson County, Tennessee, Marriage Book I*. Southern Historical Press: 1979.
Matagorda County Historical Society. *Historic Matagorda County*. Houston: D. Armstrong, Co., Inc., 1986, vol. I, pp. 32-34.
Sinks, Julia. *Chronicles of Fayette*, p. 10.

JAMES CURTIS, SR.

References:
Crozier, W. A., editor. *Spotsylvania County Records, 1721-1800*. Baltimore: Genealogical Publishing Company, 1965.
Curtis, James. File Papers and Land Record Files. Texas State Archives and General Land Office, Austin, Texas.
Daughters of the Republic of Texas. *Muster Rolls of the Texas Revolution*. Austin: DRT, Inc., 1986.
Dixon, S. H., and L. W. Kemp. *Heroes of San Jacinto*. Houston: Anson Jones Press, 1932, pp. 54, 58, 212, 221, 375.
Eddlemon, S. K., compiler. *Genealogical Abstracts From Tennessee Newspapers, 1803-1812*. Heritage Books Inc., 1989, p. 156.
Gandrud, P. J. *Marriage Records of Jefferson County, Alabama, 1818-1864*. Memphis: Milestone Press, 1979, p. 29.
Kesselus, K. *Bastrop County Before Statehood*. Austin: Jenkins Publishing Company, 1986, p. 153.

Lucus, S. E., Jr. *Mariage Book I: January 2, 1789 - December 13, 1839, Davidson County, Tennessee*. Easley, South Carolina: Southern Historical Press, 1979.

Moore, J. T. *Record of Commissions of Officers in the Tennessee Militia (1796-1815)*. Baltimore: Genealogical Publishing Company, 1977, p. 71.

Mullins, M. D. *The First Census of Texas, 1829-1836*. Washington, D. C.: National Genealogical Society, 1962, pp. 44 and 51.

Sistler B., and S. Sistler. *Tennesseans in the War of 1812*. Nashville: Byron Sistler & Associates, Inc., 1992, p. 549.

U.S. Census. 1820. Warren County, Tennessee. National Archives Microfilm M33, Roll 122.

U.S. Census. 1850. Bastrop County, Texas. National Archives Microfilm M432, Roll 908.

U.S. Census. 1860. Bastrop County, Texas. National Archives Microfilm M653, Roll 1288.

U.S. Census. 1870. Bastrop County, Texas. National Archives Microfilm M593, Roll 1574.

Williams, Villamae. *Austin's Register of Families: from the Originals in the General Land Office*. St. Louis, Missouri: Ingmire Publications, 1984.

JAMES CURTIS JR.

References:

Curtis, James, 1849-1857. Probate Index and Minute Book C: holdings of the Bastrop County Courthouse.

————. File papers. Texas State Archives. Austin, Texas.

————. Land Record Files. Texas General Land Office, Austin, Texas.

Jenkins, John H. III, editor. *Recollections of Early Texas*. Austin: The University of Texas Press, 1958, p. 157.

Kesselus, K. *Bastrop County Before Statehood*. Austin: Jenkins Publishing Company, 1986, p. 153.

Mullins, M. D. *The First Census of Texas, 1829-1836*. Washington, D. C.: National Genealogical Society, 1962, pp. 44 and 51.

U.S. Census. Bastrop County, Texas. 1850. National Archives Microfilm M432, Roll 908.

U.S. Census. Bastrop County, Texas. 1860. National Archives Microfilm M653, Roll 1288.

CHARLES DeMOSS

References:

Goodspeed's History of Southeast Missouri.

Second Census of Missouri 1803.

Settlers of Matagorda County.

Texas Census of 1826.

JOHN FOSTER

References:
1821 Smith Family Tree, in possession of T. J. Foster, Natchez, Mississippi.
Casey. *Amite County, Mississippi*. Vol. I, p. 476.
Deed Records Wilkinson County, Woodville, Mississippi.
Dunbar, Rowland. *Mississippi, Heart of the South.*
Mayes Family Bible in possession of Felix C. Kelly, Houston, Texas.
McBee, Mae Wilson. *Natchez Court Records 1767-1805*. Baltimore: Genealogical Pub. Co., 1979.
Mexican Land Grant. Texas General Land Office. Austin, Texas.
Order of the First Families of Mississippi 1699-1817, p. 72
Succession of John Foster, Probate Minutes, vol. A, p. 120, #50.
Sydnor, Charles S. *Gentleman of the Old Natchez Region*, p. 4.
Texas State Archives. Vouchers, Texas War of Independence.
Woodville Republican newspaper, volume XIV, p. 3, February 18, 1837.

RANDOLPH FOSTER

References:
Ericson, Carolyn. *First Settlers of the Republic of Texas*. St. Louis: Ingmire Publications, vol. I., 1982.
Sowell, A. J. *The History of Fort Bend County*. Houston: W. H. Coyle & Co., 1904.

CHURCHILL FULSHEAR, SR.

References:
Austin County, Texas. Succession Records.
Craven County, North Carolina. Marriage Bonds.
Fort Bend Museum. *History of Fulshear, Texas*. Richmond, Texas.
Herald Coaster [Richmond-Rosenberg, Texas], newspaper, September 1, 1972.
Houston Chronicle, newspaper, July 5, 1936. Houston, Texas.

WILLIAM GATES

References:
"Arkansas Territory." *The Pulaski County Historical Review*. Vol. XIX, pp. 384-387.
Moss, Bobby Gilmer. *The Patriots at King's Mountain*. Blacksburg, South Carolina: Scotia-Hibernia, 1990.
Robertson. *Petitions of Early Inhabitants of Kentucky to the General Assembly of Virginia 1769-1792*.

Spanish Grant of William Gates, pp. 54-57.
Starling, Edmund L. *History of Henderson County*. Kentucky Census, tax and court records.

CHESTER SPALDING GORBET

References:
Austin's 1826 Census.
Carroll, J. M. *History of Texas Baptists*. Dallas: 1923.
Fort Bend County, Texas. Probate Records.
Gorbet Papers, in possession of the family.
Pension application, dated August 1871.
Pinnell, Mrs. Sarah A. Affidavit, May 10, 1894.

COL. JARED ELLISON GROCE II

References:
Berlet, Sarah Wharton Groce. *Autobiography of a Spoon, 1828-1956*. Port Arthur, Texas: LaBelle Printing Company, 1977, pp. 96-97.
Davis, Joe Tom. *Legendary Texians*. Austin: Eakin Press, 1982, vol. III, pp. 48-63.
History of Grimes County. Retreat, Texas: n.d.
History of Waller County, Texas. 1973.
Texas Almanac, 1980-81, pp. 562-563.
Texas Parade, vol. XI, 1950.

SAMUEL C. HADDY (HADY, HEADY)

References:
Austin County, Texas. Deed Record, vol. A, pp. 49-50; Deed of Partition, Book B, p. 465.
———. Index to Deeds, p. 96.
———. Samuel C. Haddy Probate, Probate Minute Book B, pp. 55 & 170, Probate File 22(1).
Colonial Census 1820-29, Bastrop.
Texas General Land Office, Austin, Texas. Spanish Collection Box 4, Folder 30.

ALEXANDER HODGE

References:
Barker, Eugene C. *The Life of Stephen F. Austin*. Austin: 1926.
Cumberland County, Pennsylvania. Will Book, vol. B, pp. 105-106 (James Elliott's will).

Cumberland County, Pennsylvania. Will Book, vol. K, part I, p. 11 (P.O.A. by William Hodge).
Department of State. *Territorial Papers of the United States*, Vol. XIX, Arkansas Territory 181?-1825.
Elbert County, Georgia. Will Book 1791-1803, pp. 53-54 (William Hodge's will).
Harris County, Texas. Probate Book, vol. A, p. 36 (Alexander Hodge's will).
Kegans, Clarinda Pevehouse. *Memoirs*. Housed in Nita Stewart Haley Memorial Library, Midland, Texas.
Kemp, L. W. *Honor Roll of the Battle*. San Jacinto, Texas: San Jacinto Museum of History, 1974.
Oglethorpe County, Georgia. Tax Roll 1796-1805.
Texas Telegraph and Register, September 13, 1836.
Travis, William Barret. *The Travis Diary 1833-1834*. Austin: Barker Texas History Center, n.d.
University of Texas Institute of Texan Cultures. *Texas and the American Revolution*. San Antonio, Texas: 1975.

GEORGE HUFF

References:
Founders and Patriots of the Republic of Texas. Vol. II. San Antonio: Daughters of the Republic of Texas, n.d.
Geiser, S. W. *Collectors of Pleistocene Vertebrates in Early Texas (William P. Huff, 1811-1886)*. Dallas: Southern Methodist University, n.d.
Mullins, Marion Day. *The First Census of Texas 1829-1836*. Reprint. Washington, D.C.: National Genealogical Society Quarterly, 1959.
Sowell, A. J. *History of Fort Bend County*. Houston: W. H. Coyle & Co., 1904.
Texas General Land Office. Abstracts of original titles.
The Old Three Hundred: Austin's Original Colony. Waco: Texian Press.
Wharton, Clarence R. *History of Fort Bend County*. San Antonio: Naylor Company, 1939.
White, Gifford. *1840 Citizens of Texas*. Austin: 1984.
Williams, Villame. *Stephen F. Austin's Register of Families*. Baltimore: Genealogical Publishing Company, 1989.

JOHNSON CALHOUN HUNTER

References:
Goodspeed Brothers. *Memorial and Biographical Record of Southwest Texas*. Chicago 1894.
Hunter, Robert Hancock. *Narrative of Robert Hancock Hunter*. Austin: Cook Printing Company, 1936.
Red, George Plunkett. *Medicine Man in Texas*. Houston: 1930.
Sowell, A. J. *History of Fort Bend County*. Houston: W. H. Coyle & Co., 1904.

Speer, William S., and John H. Brown. *Encyclopedia of the New West*. Marshall: 1881.

SAMUEL ISAACKS

References:
Isaacks, S. J. *The Isaacks Clan in America and Texas*. El Paso: 1935.
Martin, Madeleine. *More Early Southeast Texas Families*. Quanah, Texas: Nortex Press, 1978.
Martin, Mrs. Charles. "Jasper Countians in the Army of the Republic of Texas." *Kirbyville Banner*, Kirbyville, Texas, 1971.
———. "The First to Arrive." *Kirbyville Banner*, Kirbyville, Texas, 1971.

ISAAC JACKSON, SR.

References:
Blair, E. L. *Early History of Grimes County, Texas*. Trinity: 1930.
First Census of the United States. Greene County, Georgia.
Murray, Joyce Martin. *Deed Abstracts of Washington County, Texas*. Dallas: The author, 1986.
Texas General Land Office. Certificates of Character and Applications of Land.
U.S. Census. 1850. Greene County, Georgia. National Archives Microfilm M432, Roll 71.
U.S. Census. 1850. Grimes County, Texas. National Archives Microfilm M432, Roll 910.
U.S. Census. 1880. Caldwell County, Texas. National Archives Microfilm T9, Roll 1293.
Wortham, L. J. "Wilderness to Commonwealth." *Texas Historical and Biographical Record*.

HENRY JONES

References:
Diary of Mary (Polly) Moore Jones Ryon.
Fort Bend County, Texas. Probate Record, vol. G, pp. 337-347, 417-453.
Sowell, A. J. *History of Fort Bend County*. Houston: W. H. Coyle & Co., 1904.
Steely, Skipper. *Six Months From Tennessee*. Wolfe City: 1983.
Texas General Land Office. Henry Jones land grant.

JAMES WALES JONES

References:
Dobie, J. Frank. "Jane Long Was Mother of Texas and Servants." *Fort Worth Star Telegram*, March 1, 1964.
Syers, Ed. "Off the Beaten Trail." *San Antonio Express-News*, September 3, 1965.

CAPT. RANDALL JONES

References:
Sayers, William Edward. *Off Beaten Trails*. Waco: 1971.
Texas General Land Office. Land Grants, Spanish Archives.
Texas State Library, Archives Division. Republic of Texas Pension Files.
Wharton, Clarence R. *History of Fort Bend County*. San Antonio: 1939.

BARZILLAI KUYKENDALL

References:
Texas General Land Office. Spanish Archives.
U.S. Census. 1850. Washington County, Texas. National Archives Microfilm M432, Roll 916.
U.S. Census. 1860. Washington County, Texas. National Archives Microfilm M653, Roll 1307.
Washington County, Texas. Probate Records, Book J, p. 569.

ROBERT H. KUYKENDALL

References:
Texas State Archives, Austin. "The Papers of M. B. Lamar."
Kuykendall, J. H. "The Recollection of Gibson Kuykendall." Center for American History, University of Texas at Austin.
Steely, Skipper. *Six Months from Tennessee*. Wolfe City: 1983.
Winkler, E. W. *Letters and Documents of Early Texians, 1821-1845*. Austin: 1937.

JOEL LEAKEY

References:
Lakey (Leakey) Bible records.
Leakey, Joel. Will.

Swenson, Helen. "Early Texas News."
Texas General Land Office. Two land grants to Joel Leakey signed by Stephen
F. Austin.

WILLIAM LITTLE

References:
Johnson, Frank W. *A History of Texas and Texans.* Vol. III. Chicago: 1914.
Wharton, Clarence R. *History of Fort Bend County.* San Antonio: Naylor, 1939.

NATHANIEL LYNCH

References:
Department of Texas, Atascosito District, 1826.
Harris County, Texas. Deed Records. Vol. B, p. 48; Vol. I, pp. 32-87; Vol. L,
pp. 280-318.
Texas General Land Office. Spanish Archives. Vol. 54, p. 15.

SHUBAEL MARSH

References:
Austin Papers. General Library, University of Texas, Austin.
Genealogy of the Family of George Marsh.
Hicks, Margaret Hall. *Memories of Ancestors.* Center for American History,
University of Texas, Austin.
Texas General Land Office. Spanish Archives.

ARTHUR McCORMICK

References:
Gaume, June B. McCormick. "The Battleground McCormick." Manuscript in
the possession of the author.
Johnson, Frank W. *A History of Texas and Texans.* Chicago: The American Historical Society, 1916, vol. IV, pp. 1593-1595.
"The Late Capt. Michael McCormick." *Galveston Daily News,* November 11,
1874, p. 2, col. 3.

JOHN McCROSKY

References:
Brazoria County, Texas. Court records, February 12, 1833.
Colorado County, Texas. Court records, 1832.

108

Colorado County Historical Association. *Colorado County Chronicles.* Columbus, Texas.

Justice Court, Town of San Felipe de Austin. April 12, 1825.

Kilgore, Dan E. *A Ranger Legacy.* Austin: Madrona Press, 1973, p. 73.

Matagorda County, Texas. Probate Court, October 31, 1859.

McCrosky Bible record.

"Notes and Fragments." *Southwestern Historical Quarterly*, vol. XXVI (1922-1923).

Texas General Land Office. Spanish Land Grants.

White, Emma Siggins. *Descendants of John Walker of Wiginton, Scotland*, p. 550.

JOHN H. MOORE

References:

"Come and Take It." *Washington-on-the-Brazos Quarterly*, 1981.

Des Cognets, Anne R. *William Russell and His Descendants.* Louisville, Kentucky: 1884.

DeShields, James T. *Tall Men With Long Rifles.* San Antonio: The Naylor Co., 1971.

Jones, William Moses. *Texas History in Stone.* Houston: Monument Publishing Co., 1958.

Wallace, Ernest, and David Vigness. *Documents of Texas History.* Austin: Steck Co., 1963.

WILLIAM MORTON

References:

Carter, James David. *Masonry in Texas: Background, History, and Influence to 1846.* Waco: Grand Lodge of Texas, 1955.

Court Documents from Fort Bend County, Harris County, Trinity County, Walker County, and Wharton County.

Founders and Patriots of the Republic of Texas. Vol. II. San Antonio: Daughters of the Republic of Texas, 1974.

Geiser, Samuel W. *Collectors of Pleistocene Vertebrates in Early Texas, William P. Huff (1811-86).* Dallas: Southern Methodist University.

Mullins, Marion Day. *The First Census of Texas 1829-1836.* Washington, D.C.: National Genealogical Society, 1959.

The Old Three Hundred: Austin's Original Colony. Waco: The Texian Press.

Sowell, A. J. *History of Fort Bend County.* Houston: Coyle & Co., 1904.

Texas General Land Office. Abstract of Original Titles.

Transactions Texas Lodge of Research A.F. & A.M., June 17, 1978-March 17, 1979, vol. XIV. Waco: Texas Lodge of Research, 1979.

Wharton, Clarence R. *History of Fort Bend County.* San Antonio: Naylor Company, 1939.

White, Gifford. *1840 Citizens of Texas*. Austin: Pemberton Press, 1984.
Williams, Villamae. *Stephen F. Austin's Register of Families*. Baltimore: Genealogical Publishing Co., Inc., 1989.

JOSEPH NEWMAN

References:
Austin County Courthouse, Bellville, Texas. Joseph Newman file.
Davy (Salt Creek) Cemetery, Karnes County, Texas.
History of Madison County, Illinois and county records.
Rabb, Mary Crownover. *Travels and Adventures in Texas in the 1820's*. Waco: 1962.
Texas General Land Office. 1826 Census of Austin's Colony.
Texas General Land Office. Mexican Grant #57.
Warren County, Ohio. Marriage Records.

GEORGE SAMUEL PENTECOST

References:
Fort Bend County, Texas. Deed Records. Book A, p. 140; Book, B, p. 121.
————. Probate Book A, p. 247.

DR. JAMES AENEAS PHELPS

References:
Abstract of Annual Return of Mississippi Free and Accepted Masons, 1819-1849, p. 40.
Brazoria County, Texas. Index to Probate Cases, No. 20.
Carter, James D. "The Men Who Introduced Organized Free Masonry Into Texas." *The Texas Freemason*, spring 1987.
Plunkett, Mrs. George. *The Medicine Men in Texas, Surgeons at San Jacinto*, p. 69.
Texas Forest Service. *Famous Trees of Texas*, p. 40.
Wall, Bernard. *Following General Sam Houston 1793-1863*. Houston: Clayton Library.
White, Gifford. *1840 Citizens of Texas*. Vol. II. Austin: 1984.

JOSEPH HENRY POLLEY

References:
Clapp, Marjorie. "Old Mansions Hold Ghost of Texas Past." *The Light*, San Antonio, September 13, 1955, p. 25.

Golson, Josephine Polley. *Bailey's Light*. San Antonio: Naylor, 1950, p. 65.
"Whitehall Mansion." *The Floresville Chronicle*, Floresville, Texas.
Wharton, Clarence Ray. *History of Fort Bend County*. San Antonio: Naylor, 1939.

WILLIAM PRYOR

References:
Austin County Courthouse. Austin Colony marriage records.
―――. Probate Records for William Pryor.
Mississippi Territory Census for Clarke County. 1816.
Texas General Land Office. Mexican land grant to William Pryor, Austin 300.
―――. Map of Mexican land grants.

JOHN RABB

References:
Allen, Beverly W. "Beginning of Methodism in West Texas." *West Texas Conference Journal*, 1928.
Brown, John Henry. *Indian Wars and Pioneers of Texas*. Austin: 1880.
Harper's New Monthly Magazine, vol. XXII, December 1860.
Rabb, Lillian Bell, editor. *Reminiscences of Mary Crownover Rabb*. Austin: Privately printed, Austin 1931.

CAPT. THOMAS J. RABB

References:
Brown, John Henry. *Indian Wars and Pioneers of Texas*. Austin: 1895, p. 650.
Gulick, Charles A., editor. *Lamar Papers*, vol. 4, part 1, p. 215.
Jenkins, John H., ed. *Papers of the Texas Revolution 1835-1836*. Austin: 1973, vol. III, pp. 142-144.
Kemp, Louis Wiltz, *The Signers of the Texas Declaration of Independence*. Houston: Anson Jones Press, 1944, p. 72.
Kuykendall, J. H. "Reminiscences of Early Texas." *Quarterly of the Texas State Historical Association*, vol. VI, pp. 321-324.
Memorial and Genealogical Records of Southwest Texas. Chicago: Goodspeed Brothers, 1894, pp. 337-338.
Rabb, Mary Crownover. *Travels and Adventures in Texas in the 1820's*. Waco: Morrison, 1962, pp. 1-2.
Texas General Land Office. Roll of officers of First Regiment, Texas Volunteer Army.
―――. Register of Land Titles, Folio I, p. 252.
Texas Methodist Historical Quarterly, vol. I, no. 1 (1909).
Texas Presbyterian, The. Victoria, Texas, January 2, 1847.

Texas State Library, Archives Division. Certificates of Service dated November 23, 1835, and August 29, 1836.
Webb, Walter P. *The Texas Rangers*. Cambridge: 1935.
Weyand, Leonie R., and Houston Wade. *An Early History of Fayette County*. LaGrange, Texas: LaGrange Journal, 1936, p. 124.

WILLIAM RABB

References:
Bexar Archives, Microfilm 68 for 1821.
Brown, John Henry. *Indian Wars and Pioneers of Texas*, pp. 650-651.
Chronicles of Oklahoma, p. 25.
Dunlevy, J. H., and James H. Anderson. *Dunlevy History*, p. 104.
Ellis, Thomas, ed., *History of Fayette County, Pennsylvania*, 1882.
German Township, Fayette County, Pennsylvania. Property Rolls, 1804.
Gulick, Charles A., ed. *Lamar Papers*. Vol. IV, part 1, p. 215.
History of Madison County, Illinois, 1882, p. 122.
History of Refugio County, 1836-1936, Centennial.
Kilgore, Dan. *Kilgore Express*, August 25, 1971, p. 6.
Madison County, Illinois. Courthouse Records, Book B, pp. 491, 508-509. Isaac West to William Rabb.
———. Deed Records, April 3, 1818. Wm. Rabb to Chr. Wilt.
Pennsylvania Vital Records. Will of William Scott, 1739.
Rabb, Lillian Bell. *Reminiscences of Mary Crownover Rabb*, 1931, pp. 3-4.
Smalley, Benjamin, letter to John Smalley, 10-13-1810. File No. 6, on Smalley, Rutgers University.
U.S. Archives. Military Records, War of 1812, p. 252.
Warren County, Ohio. Marriage Records, vol. I p. 12.
Wilson, Paul C. *Forgotten Mission to the Indians*, pp. 53-57.

ELIJAH ROARK

References:
Austin County papers. Charge receipt in "Elijah Roark, deceased, #38."
Brown, John Henry. *History of Texas*. St. Louis: 1892.
Center for American History. University of Texas at Austin.
Harrisburg County. Probate Records.
Quarterly of the Texas Historical Association, vol. IV, pp. 93-95.
Texas State Archives, Navarro County Records.
Texas General Land Office. Spanish Archives, Vol. I, p. 94.
Wharton, Clarence R. *History of Fort Bend County*, pp. 40-41.

NOEL FRANCIS ROBERTS

References:
Austin County Courthouse. Austin Colony marriage records.
Center for American History. The University of Texas at Austin. The 1826 Census of Austin's Colony.
Clarke County, Georgia. Marriage Register, Book A.
Daughters of Republic of Texas. Application of Jennie Mae Belt.
————. Muster Rolls of Texas Revolution.
Family story of Elizabeth Pryor Roberts walking the battlefield.
Fort Bend County probate records, George Memorial Library. Noel F. Roberts, Harriet Roberts and William Roberts.
Marriages and Deaths, 1763-1820. Abstracted from extant Georgia Newspapers by Mary Warren.
Texas General Land Office. Map of Mexican land grants.
————. Mexican land grant to Noel F. Roberts, Austin 300.

ROBERT SCOBEY

References:
Ericson, Carolyn, and Frances T. Ingmire. *Citizens of the Republic of Texas*. St. Louis: 1982.
Memorial and Biographical History of Dallas County, Texas., Chicago: Lewis Publishing Company, 1892, pp. 938-939.
Texas Gazette, January 10, 1832.

JAMES SCOTT

References:
Berkeley County, West Virginia. Deeds.
Carter, James David. *Masonry in Texas*. Waco: 1958.
Family and Bible records.
Fort Bend County, Texas. Deeds.
Frederick County, Virginia. Deeds.
Wharton, Clarence R. *History of Fort Bend County*. Houston: The Anson Jones Press, 1939.

DANIEL SHIPMAN

References:
Goliad County Historical Commission. *History and Heritage of Goliad County*, 1983.
Shipman, Daniel. *Frontier Life*. 1879.
Texas General Land Office, Austin.

MOSES SHIPMAN

References:
Harris, Dilue Rose. "The Reminiscences of Dilue Harris." *Quarterly of the Texas State Historical Association*, vol. IV, 1900-1901.
McCutchen, Joseph D. *Mier Expedition Diary*. University of Texas Press.
Texas General Land Office, Austin. Census of Austin's Colony 1826.

CAPT. BARTLETT SAMUEL SIMS

References:
Gamel, H. P. N. *Laws of Texas*. Vol. I. Austin, 1898.
McLean, Malcolm D. *Papers Concerning Robertson's Colony*. Vol. XII. Arlington: 1985.
Southwestern Historical Quarterly, Texas State Historical Association, vol. LXV, p. 291.
Texas State Library. Archives Division. Papers of Bartlett Sims.
Tolbert, Frank X. *Informal History of Texas*. New York: 1961
Watkins, Sue, ed. *One League to Each Wind*. Austin: n.d.
White, Gifford. *Character Certificates in the General Land Office*. Baltimore: 1988.

PHILLIP SINGLETON

References:
Clay County, Kentucky. Deed Book A, p. 39.
Kentucky Military Records. *Kentucky Genealogist*, vol. 22, p. 32.
Harris County, Texas. Deed Records. Vol. B, p. 103; Vol. E, p. 159.
Texas General Land Office, Austin. Land Grants.
Texas General Land Office, Austin. File C-7543.
Texas General Land Office. 1826 Census of Austin's Colony.
Wayne County, Kentucky. Green Book, p. 85.

CHRISTIAN SMITH

References:
Atascosito District Census of 1826.
Austin Colony of Pioneers (Washington County).
Early Pioneers and Settlers in Washington County.

CORNELIUS SMITH

References:
U.S. Census for Texas. 1850.
Daughters of the Republic of Texas. Dedication of Citizen of Texas Marker.
First Census of Texas (1826).
Pulaski County, Kentucky. Marriage Record.

ADAM STAFFORD

References:
Obituary. *Victoria Advocate,* November 27, 1880.
Fort Bend County, Texas. Marriage Records.
Harris, Dilue Rose. "The Reminiscences of Dilue Harris." *Quarterly of the Texas State Historical Association,* vol. IV, 1900-1901.
Stafford, Adam. Family Bible.
————. Papers, Center for American History, University of Texas at Austin.

WILLIAM STAFFORD

References:
Gulick, Charles A., and Harriet Smither, eds. *Papers of Mirabeau Buonoparte Lamar.* Vol. V. Austin: The Pemberton Press, 1968.
Harris, Dilue Rose. "The Reminiscences of Dilue Harris." *Quarterly of the Texas State Historical Association,* vol. IV, 1900-1901.
Sowell, A. J. *History of Fort Bend County.* Houston: W. H. Coyle & Co., 1904.
Stafford, Adam, Family Bible.
Wharton, Clarence R., *History of Fort Bend County.* Houston: The Anson Jones Press, 1939.
Wilson County, Tennessee. Marriage Records.

JESSE THOMPSON

References:
Fort Bend County, Texas. Court Minutes, Book A.
————. Deed Records, Book B, pp. 23-25.
Hocker, Irene Feris. Bible records.
Texas General Land Office. Land Certificate for H. C. Thompson.
Wharton, Clarence R. *Gail Borden, Pioneer.* San Antonio: 1941.
————, *History of Fort Bend County,* p. 74.

ELIZABETH TUMLINSON

References:
"Limestone Genealogy." *The Gusher*, vol. IV, no. 1. Midland County Library.
Texas General Land Office, Austin. Spanish Archives.
White, Lucille Latham. *The Tumlinsons, A Fearless Family of Gunfighters.*

JAMES WALKER, SR.

References:
Greenbriar County, West Virginia. Marriage Records.
Washington County, Texas. Deed Records.
————. Probate Records.

AMY COMSTOCK WHITE

References:
White, Gifford. *James Taylor White of Virginia.* Austin: 1982.
————. *Amy White of the Old 300.* Austin: 1986.

WILLIAM WHITLOCK

References:
Family Record of Mrs. Fannie Whitlock Sneed.
Partlow, Miriam. *Liberty, Liberty County and the Atascosito District.* Austin: The
    Pemberton Press, 1974.
St. Martin of Tours Church, St. Martinville, Louisiana. Marriages.
U.S. Census. 1850. Liberty County, Texas. National Archives Microfilm M432,
    Roll 912.
U.S. Census. 1860. Liberty County, Texas. National Archives Microfilm M653,
    Roll 1300.
White, Gifford. *1840 Citizens of Texas.* Vol. II, Tax Rolls. St. Louis: 1984.
————. *Amy White of the Old 300.* Austin: 1986. (This volume contains an
    extended history of the William Whitlock family.)

THOMAS WILLIAMS

References:
Colorado County Historical Commission. "First Census on the Colorado
    District." *Colorado County Chronicles*, 1986, vol. II, pp. 722-742.

Matagorda County Historical Commission. *Historic Matagorda County*, 1986, vol. I, pp. 103, 104.

U.S. Census. 1850. Travis County, Texas. Dwelling/Family No. 245, National Archives Microfilm M432, Roll 915.

ZADOCK WOODS

References:

Daughters of the Republic of Texas Museum and Library. *The Woods-Harrell Family.*

Spelman, Paul N. *Zadock and Minerva Cottle Woods, American Pioneers.*

Texas Historical Commision. *Guide to the Official Texas Historical Markers.*

Texas State Archives, Austin. *Republic of Texas Pension Application Abstracts.*

GLOSSARY

alcalde: served in the capacity of judge and mayor.

"Anahuac Disturbances": The disturbance of 1832 broke out as the culmination to a series of grievances of the Texas colonists. The disturbance of 1835 marked the end of a period of harmony between the settlers and the Mexican authority.

ayuntamiento: the equivalent of the modern city council.

Bexar, Siege of: preceded battle which drove the Mexican troops from Texas in December 1835.

Census of 1826: the first census of Austin's colony.

"Come and Take It" flag: This flag was flown at the Battle of Gonzales in response to the Mexican demand for the return of a cannon. See also Gonzales, Battle of.

Consultation: A body of representatives that met in San Felipe in November 1835 to discuss their situation. They decided to remain loyal citizens of Mexico but would set up a provisional government.

Convention of 1836: A group of delegates which met at Washington-on-the-Brazos, wrote the Declaration of Independence for Texas and the Constitution of the Republic, and organized the ad interim government.

empresario: a land agent or contractor used by the Mexican government to colonize Texas.

Fredonian Rebellion (1826): the first time independence from Mexico had been proclaimed in Texas.

Gonzales, Battle of: the first encounter of the Texas Revolution; see also "Come and Take It" flag.

Grass Fight: an early incident in the Siege of Bexar.

Gutierrez-Magee Expedition: an early (1812-1813), ill-fated episode in the Mexican Revolution against Spain.

land grant: the patent or title to the land granted by the government to a settler.

land terms:

hacienda	five or more square leagues.
labor	1,000,000 square *varas*, or 177.1 acres, considered the amount of tillable land for one farmer.

league   a linear measure of 5,000 *varas*; also a measure of land equal
            to a plot one league square, equal to 4428.3 acres; see also
            sitio.
sitio   one square league as needed for a ranching operation; see
            also league.
vara   a Spanish linear measure of varying value; Texas finally set-
            tled on 331/3 inches.
Lively: a schooner hired by Austin at New Orleans to bring settlers and sup-
    plies to Texas.
Mier Expedition (1842): the last of the raiding expeditions from Texas into
    Mexico during the days of the Republic of Texas; best remembered for
    the "Black Bean Episode."
Muldoon, Father Michael: a Catholic priest assigned to Austin's colony and
    known for his liberal views.
regidor: a town councilman.
Runaway Scrape: the name used for the spring 1836 flight of Texians from
    their homes to escape Santa Anna's advancing army.
sindico procurador: an official with the combined duties of notary and city
    attorney.
Texian: the term used for an Anglo-American colonist.
Velasco, Battle of (1832): preliminary to the Texas Revolution, this battle was
    the scene of the first bloodshed in relations between Texas and Mexico.
Veramendi family: a wealthy and prominent San Antonio family in colonial
    Texas.
Woll's Invasion (1842): Gen. Adrian Woll, a French mercenary, led the Mex-
    ican army in the capture of San Antonio.

TIMELINE

1821	Spain grants Moses Austin permission to bring settlers to the Province of Texas.
	Moses Austin dies.
	Mexico wins independence from Spain.
	Earliest colonists arrive in Texas.
1823	The Republic of Mexico grants Stephen F. Austin a colonization contract.
1832	Disturbance at Anahuac.
	Battle of Velasco.
1833	S. F. Austin is imprisoned in Mexico City.
1835	Austin returns to Texas.
	Trouble at Anahuac.
	Battle of Gonzales.
	Consultation, November 3.
	Grass Fight.
	Siege of Bexar.
1836	Convention, March 1.
	Declaration of Independence, March 2.
	Fall of the Alamo, March 6.
	Goliad Massacre.
	Runaway Scrape.
	Battle of San Jacinto.
	Stephen F. Austin dies.

DESCENDANTS
OF AUSTIN'S
OLD THREE HUNDRED

Descendants of Austin's Old Three Hundred

Each ancestor is listed in boldface, followed by member name and number.

Allcorn, Elijah
259   Alcorn, Audrey "Maxine"
480   Konarik, Evelyn "June" Dworsky
439   Konarik, Larry Edwin
443   Thomas, Jessie "Vera" Maddox
Allen, Martin
431   Allen, Arthur Charles, Jr.
453   Allen, Donald Sam *
451   Allen, Donald Steven
469   Allen, Troy Steven
444   Anderson, Kay Frances Allen
445   Anderson, Sheri Annette
66   Belt, Daryl Duckett
57   Belt, Walter Edwin, Jr.
152   Belt, Walter Edwin, III
68   Belt, William Jackson
15   Benton, Orville Russell
104   Byars, Lottie Fay O'Rear
103   Chiodo, Cleatis Marie O'Rear
73   Coleman, George Howard, Jr.
72   Coleman, Lucille Rumsey
2   Harrison, Katherine Allen
331   Jensen-Deign, Symantha Byars
69   Landers, Becky Jean Belt
487   McCorcle, Gary Edwin
446   Michulka, Jennifer Marie Allen
447   Michulka, Jonathan Miles
448   Penney, Laura Kay Michulka
177   Rumsey, Wallace Lloyd
511   Strauss, William Frederick
4   Stucky, Dixie Dee Benton
510   Waggoner, Mary Helen Strauss
278   Woliver, Clarence Hugh, Jr., Col. Ret.
399   Woliver, David Allen
398   Woliver, Walter Hugh
Alley, John

Alley, John C.
Alley, Rawson
Alley, Thomas V.
Alley, William A.
Alsbury, Charles G.
Alsbury, Harvey
Alsbury, Dr. Horace Arlington
Alsbury, Thomas, Jr.
    434   Miller, Katherine Pearl Lentz
    374   Whitaker, Delbert Walter
Anderson, Simeon Asa
Andrews, John
Andrews, William
    188   Ballmer, Jonette Henson
    83-S1   Duncan, Rebecca Hargrove
    58-S2   Foster, Sam Weston, Jr.
    67-S1   Lubojacky, Stephen Hampton
    244   Russell, Martha Jo Ballmer
    234   Russell, Shelly Arlene
Angier, Samuel Tubbs
    221   Patton, James Donald
    220   Patton, Nolia "Eugenia" Angier
Austin, James Elijah Brown
Austin, John
Austin, Stephen Fuller
Bailey, James Briton
    196-S1 Everts, George Bert
    400   Kolber, Jeriann Whitcomb
Balis, Daniel E.
Barnett, Thomas
    38   Fuste, Annadeil Elliott Icet *
Barrett, William
    60   Hadley, Arthur Richard
    59   Hadley, Audrey Merle Barrett *
    61   Hadley, William Melvin
    328   Moore, Joyce Elaine Speer
    62   Morgan, Deurene Oates
    63   Morgan, Tracy Diane
    329   O'Connell, Jo Ann Speer
    102   Speer, Louie Belle Barrett
    64   Wray, Dana Michele
Battle, M. M. (Mills M.)
Beard, James

Beason, Benjamin
  243   Etheridge, Bernice Elizabeth Perry
  484   Etheridge, Jodick Perry
  251   Moeller, Joann Cecilia Perry
  242   Wooten, Nancy Jane Perry
  483   Wooten, Sarah, Jane
Bell, Josiah Hughes
Bell, Thomas B.
Berry, Manders (Mandus)
Best, Isaac
  277   Bader, Eddie "Wayne"
  476   Hamilton, Odelle
Betts, Jacob
Bingham, Frances
Bloodgood, William
Boat(w)right, Thomas
  461   McKelroy, Cecilia "Joy" Boatright
Borden, Thomas Henry
Bostic, Caleb R.
Bowman, John T.
Bradley, Edward R.
  274   Peters, Doris Letitia Harrison
  477   Miller, Sylvia Seale
  455   Waites, Jacquelyn Maurice Thompson
Bradley, John
Bradley, Thomas
Breen, Charles C.
  417   Corbin, Lillian Frances Smith
  380   Jacobs, Julie Ann
  353   Jacobs, Louis Leo, Jr.
  336   Johnson, Sherrell Louise Smith
  350   Puett, Sarah B. Jacobs *
  368   Smith, Thomas Calton
  379   Sylvest, Sally Irene Jacobs
  369   Taylor, Linda Gay Jacobs
Brias (see Reels)
Bridges, William B.
  342   McElhinney, Violet Ranne
Bright, David
  23-S1   Johnson, Donna Louise McCrosky
Brinson, Enoch
Brooks, Bluford
Brotherton, Robert

126

Brown, George
Brown, John
Brown, William S.
Buckner, Aylett C.
Burnam, Jesse
      28   Higginbotham, Sarah Russell Moss
      26   Moss, Julia Nail
      27   Moss, Janice Jordan
Burnet, Pumphrey
Byrd, Micajah
      75   Howard, John Steven
    316   Mock, Vivian Lin Pollard
    263   Pollard, James Tris
    151   Schmitz, Kathleen Howard
    205   Sorsby, Kirk Morrow
    191   Sorsby, William Frederick, Sr.
Callihan, Mosis (Morris)
Calvit, Alexander
    266   Williams, Mary Elizabeth
Carpenter, David
Carson, William C.
Carter, Samuel C.
Cartwright, Jesse H.
Cartwright, Thomas N.
      13   Willhoite, Martha Lovellette
Castleman, Sylvanus
    132   Faul, Kathy Vee Woodham
Chance, Samuel
Charles, I. N. (see Nidever)
Chriesman, Horatio
Clark, John C.
Clarke, Anthony R.
Coats, Merit M.
Coles, John P.
Cook, James
Cooke, John
Cooper, William (Cow)
Cooper, William (Sawmill)
Crier, John
    229   Haecker, Mary Elizabeth Thompson
    230   Haecker, Frank August III
    231   Hamilton, Lora Jane Thompson
Crownover, John

Cumings, James
Cumings, John
Cumings, Rebekah Russel
   100   Cumings, Edward Nesbitt *
   429   Cumings, Kenneth
    36   Cumings, Louis William, III, Rev.
    18   Cumings, Timothy Austin
    37   Cumings-Jordan, Christina Marie
Cumings, William
     5   Hill, Guy Susan Cumings
Cummins, James
  28-S1   Higginbothem, Sarah R. Moss
  23-S3   Johnson, Donna Louise McCrosky
  27-S1   Moss, Janice Jorden
  26-S1   Moss, Julia Nail
Curtis, Hinton
Curtis, James, Jr.
Curtis, James, Sr.
    17   Callies, Georgia "Sue" Donovan
    16   Donovan, Dorothy D. Davis
   325   Donovan, Eugene Patrick, III
   326   Donovan, John Lyle Scott
   185   Pettit, Helen Grace Grover
   318   Reid, Charles Lee
  21-S1   Thomas, Corine Crossland
Davidson, Samuel
Davis, Thomas
Decrow, Daniel
DeMoss, Charles
   425   DeMoss, Charles Fannin, III
   138   Sanders, Allen "Hardy"
DeMoss, Peter
DeWees, William B.
Dickinson, John
Dillard, Nicholas
Duke, Thomas Marshall
Duty, George
Duty, Joseph
    65   McWhorter, Agnes McAnaney *
Dyer, Clement C.
   294   Weatherly, Hazel "Inez" Heard
Earle, Thomas
Edwards, Gustavus E.

Elam, John
Elder, Robert
Fenton, David
Fields, John F.
Fisher, James
Fitzgerald, David
Flanakin, Isaiah
Flowers, Elisha
Foster, Isaac
Foster, John
    463   Tharp, Dorothy Ruth Baker
    491   Utter, Bettie Mae Perkins
    462   Warnock, Barbara Ann Baker
    343   Zvolanek, Nadine Foster
Foster, Randolph
    48   Cowgill, Ralph Frederick "Fred"
    47   Cowgill, Winnie Rhea Wroten
    52   Edenfeld, Katrina Marie
    51   Edenfeld, Susan E. Cowgill
    58   Foster, Sam Weston, Jr.
    49   Paulson, Carolyn Elaine Cowgill
    50   Sciborski, Barbara Jean Cowgill
Frazier, James
Fulshear, Churchill, Sr.
    371   Inman, A. "Elizabeth" Johnson
    473   Kipp, Jeffrey Layne
    113   Kipp, John Emmette "Dick"
    471   Kipp, Kenneth Wayne
    472   Kipp, Michael Wayne
Furnash, Charles
Garrett, Charles
Gates, Samuel
Gates, William
    118   Armstrong, Elizabeth Lacewell
    147   Brooks, Thomas Sidney *
    173   Callaway, Oswald Elvan *
    280   Flores, Ricardo Nicolas
    281   Holmes, Barbara Elizabeth Striegler
    174   Johnston, Besta Callaway
    279   Konkle, Margaret Amabel Flores
    311   Konkle, Molly Esther
    292   McDavid, Carolyn Gates
    189   Patton, Brett Lee

19	Truitt, Barton "Brent"
9	Truitt, Cynthia Lynn
8	Truitt, Dorothy L. Butler
10	Truitt, Robert Ralph, Jr.
20	Truitt, Stephen Patrick
282	Warford, Star Irene Striegler

George, Freeman

391	Hardy, Marshel Warren *

Gilbert, Preston

Gilbert, Sarah

Gilleland, Daniel

475	Duncan, Faye Oma Darby
208	Hale, Jamie Shawn
206	Hale, Manza Lewis, Sr.
207	Hale, Manza Lewis, Jr.
252	Longmire, Lowell Kenneth
432	Scroggins, Lawrence Reginol *
319	Scroggins, Lawrence "Richard"
209	Shaw, Vanna Leigh Hale

Gorbet, Chester Spalding

341	Maddox, David Thomas
276	Maddox, Frederick Andrew
297	Maddox, Larry Allen
210	Schorr, Hattie Norene Gorbet

Gouldrich, Michael

Gray, Thomas

Groce, Jared Ellison, II

467	Bennatte, Joe Michael
211	Groce, Mary Bethany
3	Kipp, Cheryl "Sissie" Bennette

Guthrie, Robert

Haddon, John

Hady (Haddy), Samuel C.

426	Bowers, Johnanna Laxson
377	Boyd, Joanna "Jody" Vaughn Calvin
373	Calvin, Dea Bailey, Jr.
365	Calvin, Novella Vaughn *
427	Hodge, Wilma Eunice Laxson
428	Jones, Nellie Velma Laxson
430	Laxson, John Henry, III
364	Marble, Ida "Carolyn" Calvin
375	Marble, Sanford Calvin
376	Marble, Stephen Theodore

378   Marble, Stuart Laxson
372   Thornton, Georgina Vaughan
Hall, George Braxton
    482   Hall, Jody
    479   Hall, Larry Joe
    481   Jackson, Becki Laree Hall
Hall, John W.
Hall, William J.
Hamilton, David
Harris, Abner
Harris, David
Harris, John Richardson
Harris, William
Harris, William
Harris, William J.
Harrison, George
    324   Griffin, Zuleika Elizabeth Stanger
Harvey, William
Haynes, Thomas S.
Hensley, James
Hodge, Alexander
    283   Boyce, Billie "Jean" Butts
    489   Burwell, Brownie Alice Neason
    30   Crain, Marguerite Starr
    384   Eason, Inez Sutherlin
    289   Green, Angela Denice Spence
    385   Rideout, Frances Sutherlin
    25   Shaddix, Laverne Secrest
    288   Spence, Patricia Ann Franks
    490   Whitley, Lara Ann
    416   Worrell, Frances Geraldine Kegans
    287   Zschiesche, Mildred Rae Reed
Holland, Francis
Holland, William
Holliman, Kinchen
Hope, James
    390   Hightower, Colleen Ward
Hudson, Charles S.
Huff, George
    442   Klussmann, Florine Clegg Robinson
    440   Robinson, Joyce Gray Clegg
    441   Snipes, Frances Alla Robinson
Huff, John

Hughes, Isaac
Hunter, Eli
Hunter, Johnson Calhoun
    293   Beyer, Julie Christine Johnston
    337   Burnham, Suzanne L. Schoener
    222   Dudley, Frances L. "Sita" Hood
    314   Eddington, Robert Cagle
    200   Hood, Doris Lenore Williford
    240   Izzo, Dianne L. Schoener
    347   Johnston, Harris Greg, Jr.
    312   Johnston, Louis Earl
    253   Johnston, Robert Thomas
    245   Robertson, Eunice Earl Williford
    197   Schoener, Dorothy L. Williford
Iiams, John, Sr.
Ingram, Ira
Ingram, Seth
Irons, John
Isaacks, Samuel
    478   Gassett, Dorothy Reid Mathews
     55   Massingill, Tensie "Juanita" Taylor
    264   Moczygemba, Betty Jane Isaacs
    401   Verette, Mary Jane Moczygemba
Jackson, Alexander, Sr.
Jackson, Humphrey
Jackson, Isaac
    388   Dotson, Desda "Diane"
    383   Dotson, Joy Mellie Gooch
    387   Hume, Gladys Mozelle Gooch
Jamison, Thomas
Johnson, Henry W.
Jones, Henry
    403   Cline, Adoris "June" Nichols
    162   Davis, Sydney Warren, Jr.
    412   Feeny, Curtis Frederick
    392   Feeny, Virginia Lee Nichols
    409   Nichols, Curtis Stanley
    402   Nichols, Elmer Lee *
    406   Nichols, James Curtis
    161   Reading, Antoinette Davis
Jones, James Wales
    267   Antal, Laurie Ann Lee
    298   Bowen, Carol Jo Clark Baugh

Kuykendall, Robert H.
  23-S4   Johnson, Donna L. McCrosky
  29   Kuykendall, Marshall Early
League, Hosea H.
Leakey, Joel
  178   Armstrong, Evelyn Tompkins
  338   Clark, Nelwyn Ruth Lakey
  80   Foiles, Ruth Oleta Thompson
  31   Schuder, Vernon Marie Cleveland
  82   Strickland, Tommie Jean Roach
Linsey, Benjamin
Little, John Morgan
Little, William W.
  181   Morgan, V. Lynne Scarborough
  182   Murchison, Marie Scarborough
  351   Scarborough, Alfred Young, Jr.
  180   Scarborough, Bernard "Davis"
  160   Scarborough, Virginia Wessendorff Davis
Long, Jane Herbert Wilkinson
Lynch, James
Lynch, Nathaniel
  131   Keels, Flossie Stanley
  155   Ray, Marjorie M. Stanley *
Marsh, Shubael
  357   Coonly, Genevieve S. Hicks
  356   Richey, Jean Elizabeth Hicks
Martin, Wyly
Mathis, William
McClain, A. W.
McCormick, Arthur
  534   Gaume, June McCormick
McCormick, David
McCormick, John
McCoy, Thomas
McCrosky, John
  23   Johnson, Donna L. McCrosky
  22   McCrosky, John "Voss"
McFarlan, Achilles
McFarlan, John
McKinney, Thomas F.
McKinsey, Hugh
McNair, James
McNeel, Daniel

305   Christian, Anne Lee McNeel
306   Christian, Lewis S., Jr.
250   Kyle, Kathleen Michelle McNeel
411   McNeel, John Marshall, III
366   McNeel, John "Marshall," VI
247   McNeel, Linea Ann, Dr.
367   McNeel, Michael "David"
246   McNeel, Synott Lance, Sr.
249   McNeel, Synott "Lance," Jr.
248   Rapp, Peggy Janice McNeel
McNeel, George W.
McNeel, John
McNeel, John Greenville
McNeel, Pleasant D.
McNeel, Sterling
McNutt, Elizabeth
McWilliams, William
Milburn, David H.
Miller, Samuel
Miller, Samuel R.
Miller, Simon
Millican, James D.
Millican, Robert
165   Curbello, Lon Felix, Jr.
41   Rosson, Coleen Mozelle Snyder
42   Rosson, Joe Audie
Millican, William T.
Mims, Joseph
Mitchell, Asa
Monks, John L.
Moore, John Henry, Sr.
145   Fisk, Gladys Aleen Wilie
355   Hale, M. Kathleen Fisk
23-S2   Johnson, Donna L. McCrosky
Moore, Luke
Morrison, Moses
Morton, William
442-S1 Klussmann, Florine Clegg Robinson
440-S1 Robinson, Joyce Gray Clegg
441-S1 Snipes, Frances Alla Robinson
Mouser, David
Nelson, James
Newman, Joseph

146	Barron, Ferolee Joyce Newman
157	Braucht, Gladys Evelyn Newman
533-S1	Creek, Wayne Eugene
449	Dubose, Mildred Evelyn Dunn
522	Fink, Norma Jean Billings
116	Newman, Coleman Conway
143	Newman, Nicholas Conway
239	Newman, William Green
156	Newman, William "Ivan," Dr.
539-S1	Moore, Carol Ann Kuester
531-S1	Rickey, Dorothy Jean Matthew
525	Turner, Patty Newman
495-S1	Wauer, Betty J. Newman
228	Wood, Arthur Vernon
313	Wood, Gary Lynn

Nidever, Charles Isaac
Nuckols, Milton B.
Orrick, James
Osborn, Nathan
Parker, Joshua
Parker, William
Parks, William
Pennington, Isaac M.
Pentecost, George Samuel

359	Barrett, Wanda Ellen Brown
85	Beard, Amelia Josephine
86	Beard, Bonnie Ruth
457	Beard, David Ralph
84	Beard, Sidney Bertran *
88	Beard, Sidney Bertran, III
89	Beard, Tommy Andrew
423	Bell, Kenneth Russell
422	Bell, Sally Joe Brumbelow
354	Bell, Verner Lee
219	Bhatti, Clarlyn Ruth Brown
150	Boring, Patricia Marlene Kennelly
109	Bowles, Carla Sue Goldsmith
317	Boyd, Thurmond Roger
216	Brown, Clarence McFarlane
217	Brown, Doran Lamar
360	Brown, Gary Wade
169	Brown, Glenn
358	Brown, James Wade *

218	Brown, Joel Denton
382	Brown Thurmond Arnold
424	Brumbelow, Patricia Glenn
421	Brumbelow, Russell Sage
395	Callender, Doyle Gene
454	Callender, John Kennelly
394	Callender, John Randall
408	Callender, Kyle Jenkins
393	Callender, Thelma Florene Kennelly
135	Carter, Annie Lorine Weakley
225	Coffin, Jessie Carolyn Kitchen
456	Filla, Austine Beard
108	Goldsmith, Duff Marshall
105	Goldsmith, Jo Evelyn Brumbelow
362	Guajardo, Linda Kay Kennelly
149	Haas, Rebecca Shirlene Kennelly
87	Junker, Rebecca Lee Beard
361	Kennelly, Andrew Jackson
349	Kennelly, Clyde Brown, Judge
153	Kennelly, Sallie Brown *
148	Kennelly, Shirley Thurmond
223	Kitchen, Edda Mae Brown
227	Kitchen, Edward Jackson
224	Kitchen, George Allen
538	Lewis, George Russell
407	Lindsay, Cambrey Dori
396	Lindsay, Connie Gail Callender
67-S2	Lubojacky, Stephen Hampton
110	Miksch, Marian Gay Goldsmith
241	Moore, Iva Naomi Brown
136	Powell, Charlotte Fay Weakley
262	Roberts, Dorothy "Sue" Boyd
226	Roberts, Tammy Lynn Coffin
171	Robinson, Diana P. Brown
106	Roehling, Sherry Ann Goldsmith
468	Rogers, Alton Gayle
474	Rogers, Gary Zeno
170	Saman, Glenda Kay Brown
107	Schneider, Donna Goldsmith
154	Skinner, Jessie Mae Kennelly
137	Weakley, Grace Lee
134	Weakley, Grace Truet Brumbelow

Pettus, Freeman

Pettus, William
    321   Cohn, M. Lee Pettus
    323   Pettus, June
    291   White, Ruth Elizabeth "Beth"
Petty, John
Peyton, Jonathan C.
Phelps, James Aeneas E.
    235   Renaud, Aristide Frederick, Jr.
Philips, Zeno
Phillips, Isham B.
Picket, Pamela
Polley, Joseph Henry
    196   Everts, George Bert
    233   Everts, Michael Lea
Powell, Peter
Prater, William
Pruitt, Pleasant
Pryor, William
    66-S1   Belt, Daryl Ducket
    57-S1   Belt, Walter Edwin, Jr.
    152-S1   Belt, Walter Edwin, III
    68-S1   Belt, William "Jackson"
    303   Ditta, Doris Elizabeth Belt
    39-S1   Kerr, Rita Lee Roberts
    69-S1   Landers, Becky Jean Belt
    275   Marosko, Mary Kathleen "Kitty" Belt
    302   Marosko, Ronald Jon, Jr.
    493-S1   Palmiter, Jana Lynn Roberts
    488-S1   Roberts, James Edgar, III
    505-S1   Roberts, James Edgar IV
    309   Smith, Evelyn Mae Tubbs
    285-S1   Smith, Pamela Lynne Smith
    284-S1   Smith, Shirley W. Segars
    286-S1   Smith, Sue Ann
    463-S1   Tharp, Dorothy Ruth Baker
    308   Vaughn, Betty Jo Huddleston
    310   Ware, Evelyne Ann
Rabb, Andrew
Rabb, John
    129   Rabb, Lillian Bell
Rabb, Thomas J.
    114   Wegenhoft, Victor C., Col. Ret.
Rabb, William

533	Creek, Wayne Eugene
539	Moore, Carol Ann Kuester
498	Nichols, Barry Stewart
496	Nichols, Bradford Eugene
497	Nichols, Charles Brent
495	Nichols, William Wade
172	Philips, Irene Elsie Tutschke *
214	Reedy, Felicity Ann Robinson
531	Rickey, Dorothy Jean Matthew
213	Robinson, Mark Edward
504	Smith, Catherine Munson
525-S1	Turner, Patty Newman
494	Wauer, Betty J. Newman
520	Weddle, Joseph Edward
519	Weddle, William Leland
486	Young, Jo Ann Munson

Raleigh, William
Ramey, Lawrence
Randon, David
Randon, John
Rankin, Frederick Harrison
Rawls, Amos
Rawls, Benjamin
Rawls, Daniel
Reels, Patrick
Richardson, Stephen
Roark, Elijah

460	Craft, Juanita Kay Stark Grogan
452	Drake, Daniel Dwight
272	Drake, Doris A. Ballard
418	Garito, Juliette Anne LeBaron
420	Odem, Joyce Ann Moore
435	Slagle, Karen Dianne Drake

Robbins, Earle
Robbins, William

56	Burkholder, Nanetta Key
12	Keatts, Orton Gobern "Alex"

Roberts, Andrew
Roberts, Noel Francis

39	Kerr, Rita Lee Roberts
493	Palmiter, Jana Lynn Roberts
488	Roberts, James Edgar, III
505	Roberts, James Edgar, IV

492   Roberts, Lee Roy
285   Smith, Pamela Lynne Smith
284   Smith, Shirley Wilma Segars
286   Smith, Sue Ann

Roberts, William
Robertson, Edward
Robinson, Andrew
Robinson, George
Ross, James J.
San Pierre, Joseph
Scobey, Robert
113-S1   Kipp, John Emmette "Dick"

Scott, James
127   Boaz, Wanda Josephine Smith
126   Durham, Willie Mae Scott
117   Halbert, Katherine "Esther" Smith

Scott, William
Selkirk, William
Shelby, David
Shipman, Daniel
192-S1   Cunningham, Helen Irma Shipman
193-S1   Frost, Carolyn Frances Cunningham
194-S1   Nicol, Susan J. Cunningham

Shipman, Moses
192   Cunningham, Helen Irma Shipman
193   Frost, Carolyn Frances Cunningham
194   Nicol, Susan J. Cunningham

Sims, Bartlett
258   Allen, Lelia Sue Suthers
128   Moore, Joyce Jeane Avery
254   Ramp, Al 'Louise Suthers
255   Ramp, Susan Lynn
256   Sturgeon, Karlyn "Beth" Ramp
257   Suthers, Gwendoline Lenoir Robinson
21   Thomas, Corine Crossland

Singleton, George Washington
433   Fox, Vera "Dee" Morris Smith

Singleton, Philip
112   Anders, Donald Ray
119   Anders, James Wyatt
111   Anders, Victor Henry, Jr.
260   Caffall, Thomas Henry "Jack"
261   Caffall, Thomas Henry, III

78	Domingue, Dorothy Oates
90	Evans, Ann Eulalie Oates
124	Kauffman, Ellen Kay Stedman
79	Oates, Marion Arietta *
330	Owens, Bertha Luella Oates
81	Owens, Ruby Leona Oates
53	Stedman, Shirley J. Hanagriff
123	Stedman, Wyatt Kendall
91	Stewart, Marguerite Faye Oates

Smith, Christian

140	Blanton, Rosedawn Wilbourn
527	Keith, Arleta June Bowles
517	Luther, Marilyn Clair Roeller
518	Luther, Paul Thomas
142	May, Rose Mae Shannon
176	McBee, Charles Douglas, Jr.
528	Monahan, Douglas Wayne
141	Wilbourn, Evelyn M. Shannon

Smith, Cornelius

| 139 | Henderson, Iantha "Maxine" Moses |

Smith, John

Smithers (Smothers, Smeathers), William

509	Berkebile, Joyce Marie Munson
333	Hall, Joel McClure
304	Hall, M. Louise Smothers
332	Hall, Steven Michael
352	Ponton, Fannie Hiburnia "Bernie" Munson

Snider, Gabriel Straw

Sojourner, Albert Lloyd

Spencer, Nancy

Stafford, Adam

| 215-S1 | Campbell, Wincie Marie Chenault |
| 238-S1 | Chenault, Marie Estell Clark * |

Stafford, William Joseph

| 215 | Campbell, Wincie Marie Chenault |
| 238 | Chenault, Marie Estell Clark * |

Stevens, Thomas

Stout, Owen H.

Strange, James

Sutherland, Walter

Tally, David

Taylor, John D.

Teel, George W.

Thomas, Ezekiel
   386   Francis, Blanche Nell Peters Tevis
Thomas, Jacob
Thompson, Jesse
   334   Campbell, Linda Joy Wilkerson
   125   Lubojacky, Jo Ann Bailey
    67   Lubojacky, Stephen Hampton
   121   McDowell, Lisa Carol Lubojacky
   163   Smith, Frances Cornelia Thompson
   327   Van Ordstrand, Alice Virginia Thompson
Tone, Thomas J.
Tong, James F.
Toy, Samuel
Trobough, John
Tumlinson, Elizabeth Plemmons
   212   Autry, John Franklin
   354   Bell, Verner Lee
   158   Blakeway, Annette Tumlinson
   508   Brown, James Michael
    24   Cammack, Ruth Estelle Reed
   175   Dent, Margaret Gould
   300   Haddon, Joyce Ann Reimschissel
   307   Hall, Sally Patricia Carr
   521   Hardy, Marjorie Mae Moss
   115   Harkey, Joyce Annette Carr
    74   Hays, Nadine Frances Dees
   133   Kirkscey, Bena Ray Taylor
   537   Lowther, Georgia Catherine Vann
   187   McCauley, Constance Joy Stark
   159   Meine, Vina Mae Tumlinson
   464   Moore, Charlsie Mae English
   485   Murdock, Sammie Lee
   523   Pollard, Edwin Lloyd, Jr.
   524   Pollard, Stephen Alan
   301   Reimschissel, Charlie Hugo, Jr.
   470   Reimschissel, David Wayne
   299   Reimschissel, Mary Louise Acord
   179   Sucke, Mary Winthrop Warren
   500   Upton, William Travis
   506   Wheeless, Georgia Mae Winn
   507   Winn, Charles Thomas
Tumlinson, James, Jr.
   335   Blackstone, Sandra Deanne Cain

348   Clayton, Sharron Dianne Cain
Van Dorn, Isaac
Varner, Martin
Vince, Allen
Vince, Richard
Vince, Robert
Vince, William
Walker, James, Sr.
450   Boothe, Ruby "Marie" Lindsey
201   Creel, Georgia Jane Grubb
295   Davis, Betty Sue Walker
265   Hale, June Panton
203   Holmes, Ada Eleanor Johnson
204   Johnson, Lloyd Seamon *
499   Johnson, Norma Louise Lindsey
296   Love, Gladys Marie Walker
199   Ramsey, Charlie Glen Johnson
436   Simpson, Vera Oleta Lindsey
202   Smith, Zenda Ruth Johnson
271   Thacker, Marilyn Ruth Walker *
459   True, Ina Mozelle Walker
Walker, Thomas
Wallace, Caleb
Wells, Francis Flournoy
515   Byrd, David Harold, III
514   Byrd, Roberta Adele Brackenridge Menger
516   Caruth, Adele Leigh
513   Caruth, Owene Brackenridge Peeler Crutcher Menger
512   Menger, Johnowene Brackenridge Peeler Crutcher
Westall, Thomas
White, Amy Comstock
167   Bruce, Thomas Howard
166   Bruce, William Thomas, Jr.
46-S1   Maxfield, Rose "Mary" Stiarwalt
144   Purdy, Catherine C. Bruce
40   White, Gifford E.
White, Joseph
White, Reuben
White, Walter C.
White, William C.
Whitesides, Boland
Whitesides, Henry
Whitesides, James W.

Whitesides, William B.
Whiting, Nathaniel
Whitlock, William
   315   Blair, Mary Patricia "Pat" Maxfield
    99   Maxfield, Mary Constance "Connie"
    46   Maxfield, Rose "Mary" Stiarwalt
   397   Weibruch, Marilyn Joan Maxfield
Wightman, Elias D.
Wilkins, Jane
Williams, George I.
Williams, Henry
Williams, John
Williams, John
Williams, John R.
Williams, Robert H.
Williams, Samuel May
   322   Harshman, Walter Neill, Jr.
Williams, Solomon
Williams, Thomas
   532   Rusk, Betty Jo Ray
Woods, Zadock
   389   Baker, M. Lounell Wagoner
   236   Bell, Neva Frances Harrell
    11   Brantley, Harold Clayton, Sr.
    97   Brinson, Karen E. Roach
   414   Crowl, Leesa Ellen Hahn
   410   Davies, Elizabeth Brantley Durham
   536   Deason, Jay Warren
   535   Deason, Marian (Mary) Maxine Duderstadt
   419   Durham, Andrew David
   164   Durham, David Ross
   404   Durham, Marshall Pershing, Jr.
   405   Durham, Wendy Hanks
    94   Durham, Zoie Avanell Brantley
   363   Elgin, Laurinda Rae Hall Thomas
   340   Frazier, Joel Edward
   415   Hahn, Anson Justin
   413   Hahn, Jack Burton
    35   Harrell, Hollis R. *
    70   Harison, Virginia R. Niemeier
    45   Harvey, Elizabeth Nuinez
   232   Hatcher, Mary Joyce Mobley *
   503   Hill, Ann Glimp *

34	Isley, Doris Lee Niemeier
437	Koehl, Rose Olivia Gilliam *
98	Laing, Leslie Carol Roach
501	Lewis, Doris Glimp
122	Little, Marianne Elizabeth Hall
237	McGuigan, Alma "Fern" Green
76	Moore, Linda Carolyn Ralls
502	Mullens, Diane Lewis
33	Niemeier, Rose Block *
438	Norton, Patsy Loyce Ann Gilliam
44	Nuinez, Joe Edward, Jr.
43	Nuinez, Tommie Spellman
32	Parr, Reed Brantley
458	Pass, Sharon Fredericka Baker
77	Reinecke, Lillian C. Mueller
95	Roach, Andrew Jackson
186	Saulnier, Amy Ann Brown
71	Schendel, Beth Ann Niemeier
273	Tidwell, M. "Jean" Brantley
96	Waxman, Andrea S. Roach
339	Williams, Dinah Lee Frazier
530	Woods, Ronald Roy
54	Woolsey, Elnora Frazier

* Deceased

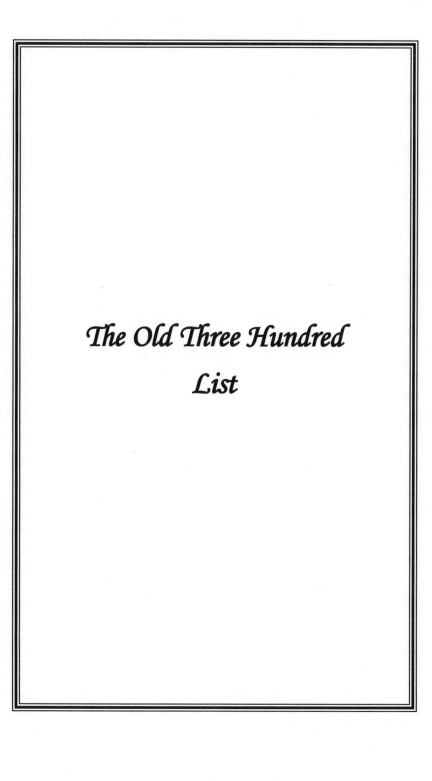

The Old Three Hundred List

THE OLD THREE HUNDRED

The colonists who settled under the terms of Austin's first contract came to be known as "The Old Three Hundred," because the contract was for the introduction of 300 families. The actual number of families introduced under it, however, was 297. Nine families received two titles each. The table given below is an adaptation of one compiled from the records of the General Land Office at Austin, Texas, by Lester G. Bugbee, and published in the *The Quarterly of the Texas State Historical Association* for October 1897 (Volume I). It gives the names of the colonists, the amount of land received by each, the present county in which the land is located, and the date that the title was issued. A *labor* of land was about 177 acres, and a *sitio*, or league, about 4,428 acres.

NAME	AMOUNT OF LAND		PRESENT LOCATION	DATE OF TITLE
	sitios	*labors*		
Allcorn, Elijah	1		Fort Bend	July 10, 1824
	½		Washington	July 10, 1824
		1	Waller	July 10, 1824
Allen, Martin	1		Wharton	July 19, 1824
		1	Austin	July 19, 1824
Alley, John	1		Jackson & Lavaca	May 14, 1827
Alley, John	1		Fayette	May 16, 1827
Alley, Rawson	1½		Colorado	Aug. 3, 1824

Name	No.	County	Date
Alley, Thomas	1	Brazoria	July 29, 1824
Alley, William			
Alsbury, Charles G.			
Alsbury, Harvey	1½	Brazoria	Aug. 3, 1824
Alsbury, Horace			
Alsbury, Thomas	2	Fort Bend & Brazoria	July 8, 1824
	1½	Waller	July 8, 1824
Anderson, S. A.	1	Fayette	Aug. 10, 1824
Andrews, John	1	Fayette & Colorado	July 7, 1824
		Waller	July 7, 1824
Andrews, William	1	Fort Bend	July 15, 1824
	1	Fort Bend	July 15, 1824
Angier, Samuel T.	1	Brazoria	Aug. 16, 1824
		Brazoria	Aug. 24, 1824
Austin, John	2	Harris	July 21, 1824
	1	Brazoria	Aug. 24, 1824
Austin, Santiago E. B.	3	Brazoria	Aug. 19, 1824
		Brazoria	Aug. 19, 1824
Austin, Santiago B.	1	Waller	Aug. 24, 1824
Austin, Estevan F.	5	Brazoria	Sept. 1, 1824
	7½	Brazoria	Sept. 1, 1824
	⅓	Brazoria	Sept. 1, 1824
	½	Brazoria	Sept. 1, 1824
	¼	Brazoria	Sept. 1, 1824
	1¾	Brazoria	Sept. 1, 1824
	2⅙	Brazoria	Sept. 1, 1824

Name		County	Date
(Austin, Estevan F.)	3/6	Wharton	Sept. 1, 1824
	2	Wharton	Sept. 1, 1824
	3	Brazoria	Sept. 1, 1824
Baily, James B.	1	Brazoria	July 7, 1824
Balis, Daniel E.	1	Matagorda	April 14, 1828
Baratt, William	1	Fort Bend	June 4, 1827
Barnet, Thomas	1	Fort Bend	July 10, 1824
Battle, M. M.	1	Matagorda	Aug. 10, 1824
Battle, Mills M.	1	Fort Bend	May 31, 1827
Beard, James	1	Fort Bend	Aug. 10, 1824
Beason, Benejani	1	Colorado	Aug. 7, 1824
Belknap, Charles	1	Fort Bend	May 22, 1827
Bell, Josiah H.	1½	Brazoria	Aug. 7, 1824
Bell, Thomas B.	1	Brazoria	Aug. 16, 1824
Berry, M.		(Partner of M. M. Battle)	
Best, Isaac	1	Waller	Aug. 19, 1824
Betts, Jacob	1	Matagorda	Aug. 19, 1824
Biggam, Fras	1	Wharton	July 10, 1824
	1	Brazoria	July 10, 1824
	1	Waller	July 10, 1824
Bloodgood, Wm.	1	Chambers & Harris	Aug. 10, 1824
Boatwright, Thomas	1	Austin	July 27, 1824
Borden, Thos.	1	Brazoria	July 29, 1824
Bostick, Caleb R.	1	Matagorda	July 24, 1824
Bowman, John T.	1	Matagorda	Aug. 21, 1824
Bradley, Edward R.	1	Brazoria	Aug. 10, 1824

Name	No.	Location	Date
Bradley, John	1	Brazoria	July 8, 1824
Bradley, Thomas		(Partner of S. T. Angier)	
Breen, Charles	1	Brazoria	May 24, 1824
Brias, Patrick	1	Harris	May 1, 1827
Bridges, Wm. B.	1	Jackson	July 21, 1824
Bright, David	1	Fort Bend	July 15, 1824
		Austin	July 15, 1824
Brinson, Enoch	1	Harris	Aug. 7, 1824
Brooks, Bluford	1	(Forfeited)	Aug. 10, 1824
Brotherington, Robt.		(Partner of Caleb R. Bostick)	
Brown, George		(Partner of Charles Belknap)	
Brown, John	1	Harris	Aug. 19, 1824
	1	Waller	Aug. 19, 1824
Brown, William S.	1	Washington	July 29, 1824
Buckner, Aylett C.	1	Matagorda	July 24, 1824
	2	Matagorda	Aug. 24, 1824
Burnet, Pumphrey	1	Matagorda	July 24, 1824
Burnam, Jesse	1	Fayette	Aug. 16, 1824
	1	Colorado	Aug. 16, 1824
Byrd, Micajah	1	Washington	July 16, 1824
Calliham, Mosis A.	1	Harris	Aug. 3, 1824
Calvit, Alexr.	1	Brazoria	Aug. 3, 1824
	1	Waller	Aug. 3, 1824
	1	Brazoria	Aug. 3, 1824
Carpenter, David	1	Harris	Aug. 16, 1824
Carson, Wm. C.	1	Brazoria	May 15, 1827

Name			Location	Date
Carter, Saml.	1		Brazoria	July 8, 1824
Cartwright, Jesse H.	1	1	Fort Bend	Mar. 31, 1828
			Lavaca	Mar. 31, 1828
Cartwright, Thomas	1	1	Colorado	Aug. 10, 1824
			Austin	Aug. 10, 1824
Castleman, Sylvenus	2	2	Wharton	July 7, 1824
	½		Fayette	July 7, 1824
			Austin	July 7, 1824
Chance, Samuel	1		Brazoria	July 27, 1824
Charles, Isaac N.	1		Brazoria	May 21, 1827
Chriesman, Horatio	1	2	Fort Bend	July 8, 1824
			Austin	July 8, 1824
Clark, John C.	1		Wharton	July 16, 1824
Clarke, Antony R.	1	1	Brazoria	Aug. 24, 1824
Coats, Merit M.	1		Waller	July 19, 1824
Coles, Jno. P.	7½		Burleson & Washington	Aug. 19, 1824
	½		Washington	Aug. 19, 1824
	½		Brazoria	Aug. 19, 1824
Cook, James	1		Colorado	Aug. 3, 1824
Cooke, Jno.	1		(Partner of Isaac Hughes)	
		1	Harris	Aug. 10, 1824
				Aug. 10, 1824
Cooper, William	1		Matagorda	July 24, 1824
Cooper, William	1½	2	Waller	Aug. 10, 1824
			Austin	Aug. 10, 1824
Crier, John	1		Matagorda	June 6, 1827
Crownover, John	1		Wharton & Matagorda	Aug. 3, 1824

Name		County	Date
(Crownover, John)		Austin	
Cummings, James	1	Brazoria	Aug. 16, 1824
	5	(Forfeited)	Aug. 16, 1824
Cummings, John	1	Brazoria	July 21, 1824
Cummings, Rebecca	1	Brazoria	July 21, 1824
	2	Waller	July 21, 1824
Cummings, William	1	Brazoria	July 21, 1824
Cummins, James	1	Colorado	July 7, 1824
	5	Austin	July 7, 1824
	1	Colorado	July 7, 1824
Curtis, Hinton	1	Matagorda	Aug. 10, 1824
Curtis, James Sr.	1	Burleson	Aug. 3, 1824
Curtis, James Jr.	1	Brazos	Aug. 19, 1824
Davidson, Samuel	1	Brazos	July 21, 1824
Davis, Thomas	1	Austin	July 29, 1824
Deckrow, D.	1	Matagorda	July 24, 1824
Demos, Charles	1	Matagorda	Aug. 3, 1824
Demos, Peter	1	Matagorda	
Dewees, Wm. B.		(Partner of James Cook)	
Dickinson, John	1	Galveston & Harris	Aug. 19, 1824
Dillard, Nicholas	1	Brazoria	Aug. 16, 1824
Duke, Thomas M.	1	Matagorda	July 24, 1824
Duty, George	1	Fayette	July 19, 1824
Duty, Joseph	1	Colorado	July 19, 1824
Dyer, Clement C.	1	Colorado	Aug. 10, 1824
	1½	Waller	Aug. 24, 1824

Name		County	Date
Earle, Thos.	1	Harris	July 7, 1824
	1	Harris	July 7, 1824
Edwards, G. E.		Wharton	Aug. 19, 1824
Elam, John	1	(Forfeited)	Aug. 7, 1824
Elder, Robert	1	Waller	Aug. 7, 1824
Falenash, Charles	1	Burleson	Aug. 19, 1824
Fenton, David	1	Matagorda	July 29, 1824
Fields, John F.	1	Brazoria	Aug. 24, 1824
Fisher, James	1	Burleson	July 19, 1824
Fitzgerald, David	1	Fort Bend	July 10, 1824
Flanakin, Isaiah	2	Austin	July 19, 1824
Flowers, Elisha	1	Matagorda	July 19, 1824
		Colorado	July 19, 1824
Foster, Isaac	1	Matagorda	Aug. 10, 1824
Foster, John	2½	Fort Bend	July 15, 1824
	3	Fort Bend	July 15, 1824
Foster, Randolph	1	Waller & Fort Bend	July 16, 1824
Frazier, James	1	Austin & Fort Bend	July 24, 1824
Fulshear, Charles	1	Fort Bend	July 16, 1824
Garret, Charles	1	Brazoria	July 15, 1824
	1	Waller	July 15, 1824
Gates, Samuel	½	Washington	July 8, 1824
	½	Washington	July 8, 1824
Gates, William	1	Washington	July 16, 1824
	1	Washington	July 16, 1824
George, Freeman	1	Matagorda	July 7, 1824

Name		Location	Date
(George, Freeman)		Waller	July 7, 1824
Gilbert, Preston	1	Colorado	June 4, 1827
Gilbert, Sarah		Wharton & Fort Bend	May 11, 1827
Gilleland, Daniel	1	Austin	Aug. 3, 1824
Gorbet, Chester S.	1	Brazoria	July 19, 1824
Gouldrich, Michael	1	Galveston	Aug. 24, 1824
Gray, Thos.	1	Brazoria	Aug. 16, 1824
		Colorado	Aug. 16, 1824
Groce, Jared E.	5	Brazoria	July 29, 1824
	2	Waller	July 29, 1824
	3	Grimes	July 29, 1824
Guthrie, Robert	1	Jackson	July 19, 1824
Haddan, John	1	Colorado	July 29, 1824
Hady, Samuel C.	1	Waller	Aug. 19, 1824
Hall, Geo. B.		(Partner of Samuel T. Angier)	
Hall, John W.	2	Brazoria	July 10, 1824
	2	Waller	July 10, 1824
Hall, W. J.	1	Fort Bend	July 10, 1824
Hamilton, David	1	Wharton	May 9, 1827
Harris, Abner	1	(Partner of William Baratt)	
Harris, David	1	Harris	Aug. 19, 1824
Harris, John R.	1	Harris	Aug. 16, 1824
Harris, William		(Partner of David Carpenter)	
Harris, William	1	Brazoria	July 10, 1824
Harris, William J.	1	Harris	July 21, 1824
Harrison, George	1	Brazoria	Aug. 16, 1824

156

Name			County	Date
Harvey, William	1		Austin	July 20, 1824
Haynes, Thomas S.	1		Brazos	Aug. 16, 1824
Hensley, James	1		Brazoria	Aug. 3, 1824
		1	Austin	Aug. 3, 1824
Hodge, Alexander	1		Fort Bend	April 12, 1828
Holland, Francis	1		Grimes	Aug. 10, 1824
Holland, William	1		Grimes	Aug. 10, 1824
Holliman, Kinchen	1		(Forfeited)	Aug. 10, 1824
Hope, James	1		Brazos	July 10, 1824
	¼	2	Brazos	July 10, 1824
				July 10, 1824
Hudson, C. S.	1		Wharton	July 29, 1824
Huff, John	1		Wharton	July 10, 1824
Huff, George	1½		Wharton & Fort Bend	Aug. 19, 1824
Hughes, Isaac			(Partner of John Cooke)	(Forfeited)
Hunter, Eli	1		Wharton	July 24, 1824
Hunter, Johnson	1		Harris	Aug. 10, 1824
Iiams, John	1		Chambers	Aug. 7, 1824
Ingram, Ira	1	1	Waller	Aug. 24, 1824
Ingram, Seth	2	1	Wharton	July 29, 1824
			Austin	July 29, 1824
Irons, John	1		Waller	July 16, 1824
Isaacks, Samuel	1		Fort Bend	July 15, 1824
Jackson, Alexander	2		Wharton	July 16, 1824
Jackson, Humphrey	1		Harris	Aug. 16, 1824
			Harris	Aug. 16, 1824

Name		Location	Date
Jackson, Isaac	1	Grimes	Aug. 7, 1824
Jamison, Thomas	1	Matagorda & Brazoria	July 24, 1824
Johnson, Henry W.		(Partner of Thos. H. Borden)	
Jones, Henry	1	Fort Bend	July 8, 1824
Jones, J. W.	1	Wharton	Aug. 10, 1824
	1	Fort Bend	Aug. 10, 1824
Jones, Oliver	1	Brazoria	Aug. 10, 1824
	1	Austin	Aug. 10, 1824
Jones, R.	½	Wharton	July 15, 1824
	½	Fort Bend	July 15, 1824
	1	Fort Bend	July 15, 1824
Keep, Imla	1	Brazoria	July 24, 1824
Keller, John C.	1	Matagorda	June 4, 1827
Kelly, John	2	Brazos	July 19, 1824
Kennedy, Sam'l	1	Fort Bend	July 7, 1824
	1	Austin	July 7, 1824
Kennon, Alfred	1	Burleson	July 19, 1824
Kerr, James	1	Jackson	May 6, 1827
Kerr, Peter			
Kerr, William	1	Washington	Aug. 10, 1824
Kincheloe, William	1	Wharton	July 8, 1824
	1	Wharton	July 8, 1824
Kingston, William	1	Matagorda	May 8, 1827
Knight, James	1	Fort Bend	July 15, 1824
	1	Fort Bend	July 15, 1824

Name			Location	Date
Kuykendall, Abner	1		Fort Bend	July 7, 1824
	½		Washington	July 7, 1824
		2	Austin	July 7, 1824
Kuykendall, Brazilla		1	Austin	Aug. 7, 1824
Kuykendall, Joseph	1		Fort Bend	July 8, 1824
Kuykendall, Robert	1		Wharton	
			Wharton	
League, Hosea H.	1		Matagorda	May 25, 1827
Leakey, Joel	1		Washington & Austin	May 28, 1827
Linsey, Benjamin	1		(Forfeited)	Aug. 19, 1824
Little, John	1		Austin	May 21, 1828
		1	Fort Bend	May 21, 1828
Little, William	1		Fort Bend	July 10, 1824
		1	Fort Bend	July 10, 1824
Long, Jane H.	1		Fort Bend	April 30, 1827
			Waller	May 1, 1827
Lynch, James	1		Washington	July 16, 1824
Lynch, Nathaneal	1		Harris	Aug. 19, 1824
McCroskey, John	1		Brazoria	Aug. 16, 1824
		1	Austin	Aug. 16, 1824
McCormick, Arthur	1		Harris	Aug. 10, 1824
McCormick, David	1		Brazoria	July 21, 1824
McCormick, John			(Partner of James Frazier)	
McCoy, Thomas			(Partner of Daniel Deckrow)	
McFarlan, Aechilles	1½		Brazoria	July 10, 1824
			Waller	July 10, 1824

159

Name			County	Date
McFarlan, John	1¼	1	Waller	Aug. 10, 1824
			Waller	Aug. 10, 1824
McKenney, Thos. F.	1		Brazos	Aug. 16, 1824
McKinsey, Hugh	1		Wharton & Matagorda	Aug. 3, 1824
McClain, A. W.				
McNair, James	1		Colorado	July 24, 1824
McNeel, Daniel	1		Brazoria	Aug. 3, 1824
McNeel, George W.	½		Brazoria	Aug. 10, 1824
McNeel, John G.	½		Brazoria	Aug. 10, 1824
McNeel, John	1		Brazoria	Aug. 3, 1824
McNeel, Pleasant D.	1		Brazoria	Aug. 7, 1824
McNeel, Sterling	1		Brazoria	Aug. 19, 1824
McNutt, Elizabeth	1		Jackson	July 21, 1824
McWilliams, William	1		Burleson	July 19, 1824
Marsh, Shubael	1		Brazoria	July 8, 1824
Martin, Wily	1		Brazoria	July 29, 1824
Mathis, William	1		Brazos	July 19, 1824
Milburn, David H.			(Partner of Thomas Davis)	
Miller, Samuel	1		Washington	Aug. 19, 1824
Miller, Samuel R.	1		Washington	Aug. 19, 1824
Miller, Simon	1		Fort Bend	Aug. 7, 1824
Millican, James D.	1		Brazos	July 16, 1824
Millican, Robert	2½		Brazos	July 16, 1824
Millican, William	1		Brazos	July 16, 1824
Minus, Joseph	1		Brazoria	Aug. 19, 1824

Name		Location	Date
Mitchell, Asa	1	Brazoria	July 7, 1824
	½	Brazoria	July 7, 1824
		Brazoria	Aug. 24, 1824
Monks, John L.	1	(Forfeited)	
Moore, John H.		(Partner of Thomas Gray)	
Moore, Luke	1	Harris	Aug. 3, 1824
Morrison, Moses		(Partner of William Cooper)	
Morton, William	1½	Fort Bend	July 15, 1824
	1	Fort Bend	July 15, 1824
Mouser, David	1	Waller	Aug. 19, 1824
Nelson, James	1	Colorado	Aug. 7, 1824
Newman, Joseph	1	Wharton	Aug. 10, 1824
		Austin	Aug. 10, 1824
Nuckols, M. B.	1	Matagorda & Brazoria	Aug. 3, 1824
	1	Brazoria	Aug. 3, 1824
Orrick, James	1	Austin	Aug. 10, 1824
Osborn, Nathan	1	Colorado	July 24, 1824
Parks, Wm.			
Parker, Joshua	1	Wharton	July 24, 1824
Parker, William	1	Brazoria	July 8, 1824
		Waller	July 8, 1824
Pennington, Isaac	1	Fort Bend	Aug. 3, 1824
Pentecost, George S.	1	Matagorda	Aug. 19, 1824
Pettus, Freeman	1	Colorado & Fayette	Aug. 3, 1824
	1	Matagorda & Brazoria	Aug. 3, 1824
		Colorado	Aug. 3, 1824

Name		County	Date
Pettus, William	1	Wharton	July 10, 1824
	1	Fort Bend	July 10, 1824
	1	Waller	July 10, 1824
Petty, John	1	Fayette	Aug. 10, 1824
Peyton, J. C.	1	Matagorda	May 25, 1827
Phelps, James A. E.	1	Brazoria	Aug. 16, 1824
	2	Brazoria	Aug. 16, 1824
Philips, I. B.	1	Wharton	May 9, 1827
Philips, Zeno	1	Brazoria	July 19, 1824
Picket, Pamelia	1	Matagorda	July 21, 1824
	1	Austin	July 21, 1824
Polley, Joseph H.		(Partner of Samuel Chance)	
Polley, Joseph H.	1	Fort Bend	Aug. 16, 1824
Powell, Peter		(Partner of William Kingston)	
Prater, William	1	Brazoria	July 19, 1824
	1	Austin	July 19, 1824
Pruitt, Pleasant	1	Matagorda	July 24, 1824
Pryor, William	1	Waller	Aug. 24, 1824
Rabb, Andrew	1½	Wharton	Aug. 10, 1824
Rabb, John	1	Fort Bend	July 8, 1824
	2	Austin	July 8, 1824
Rabb, Thomas J.	1	Wharton	July 24, 1824
Rabb, William	3	Fayette	July 19, 1824
	2	Matagorda	July 19, 1824
	2	Fayette	Aug. 24, 1824
Raleigh, William	1	Burleson	Aug. 16, 1824

Name		Location	Date
Ramey, L.	1	Matagorda	May 23, 1827
Randon, David		(Partner of Isaac Pennington)	
Randon, John	1	Fort Bend	Aug. 19, 1824
Rankin, Frederic H.	1	Harris	July 7, 1824
		Harris	July 7, 1824
Rawls, Amos	1	Matagorda	July 24, 1824
Rawls, Benjamin	1	Matagorda	Aug. 3, 1824
Rawls, Daniel	1¼	Matagorda	July 24, 1824
Richardson, Stephen	1	Brazoria	July 10, 1824
Roark, Elijah	1	Fort Bend	July 10, 1824
		Waller	July 10, 1824
Robbins, Earle	1	Austin	July 19, 1824
Robbins, William	1	Brazoria	July 19, 1824
		Austin	July 19, 1824
Roberts, Andrew	1	Fort Bend	May 11, 1827
Roberts, Noel F.	1¼	Fort Bend	July 15, 1824
Roberts, William	1	Brazoria	July 8, 1824
Robertson, Edward		Fort Bend	Mar. 31, 1828
Robinson, A.	1½	Brazoria	July 8, 1824
	½	Washington	July 8, 1824
	1	Waller	July 8, 1824
Robinson, Geo.	1	Brazoria	July 8, 1824
Ross, James	1	Colorado	July 19, 1824
San Pierre, Joseph	1	Fort Bend	Aug. 24, 1824
Scobey, Robert	1	Wharton	Aug. 3, 1824
Scott, James	1	Fort Bend	Aug. 7, 1824

163

Name		Location	Date
Scott, Wm.	1	Harris	Aug. 19, 1824
	1	Harris	Aug. 19, 1824
		Harris	Aug. 19, 1824
Selkirk, William	1	Matagorda	Aug. 10, 1824
Shelby, David		(Partner of John McCormick)	
Shipman, Daniel		(Partner of Isaac N. Charles)	
Shipman, Moses	1	Fort Bend	July 19, 1824
	1	Austin	July 19, 1824
Sims, Bartlet	1	Wharton	Aug. 7, 1824
Singleton, G. W.	1	Wharton	May 14, 1827
Singleton, Philip	1	Burleson & Washington	Aug. 19, 1824
Smith, Christian	1	Harris & Chambers	July 19, 1824
Smith, Cornelius	1	Brazoria	Aug. 10, 1824
Smith, John		(Partner of Hugh McKinsey)	
Smeathers, William	1	Austin	July 16, 1824
Snider, Gabriel S.	1	Colorado	Aug. 7, 1824
Sojourner, Albert L.		(Partner of Pumphrey Burnet)	
Spencer, Nancy	1	Fort Bend	Aug. 19, 1824
Stafford, Adam	1	Waller	Aug. 24, 1824
Stafford, William	1½	Fort Bend	Aug. 16, 1824
	1	Waller	Aug. 16, 1824
Stevens, Thomas	1	Waller	Aug. 7, 1824
Stout, Owen H.		(Partner of Benjamin Rawls)	
Strange, James	1	Harris	Aug. 24, 1824
Sutherland, Walter	1	Brazos	Aug. 10, 1824
Talley, David	1	Brazoria	Aug. 16, 1824

Name		County	Date
(Talley, David)	1	Austin	Aug. 16, 1824
Taylor, John I.	1	Harris	Aug. 10, 1824
Teel, George	1	Fort Bend	Aug. 3, 1824
Thomas, Ezekiel	1	Harris	Aug. 19, 1824
Thomas, Jacob	1	Waller	Aug. 24, 1824
Thompson, Jesse	1	Brazoria	Aug. 7, 1824
Tone, Thomas J.		(Partner of Thomas Jamison)	
Tong, James F.	1	Brazoria	Aug. 19, 1824
Toy, Samuel	1	Austin	May 7, 1827
Trobough, John		(Partner of Patrick Brias)	
Tumlinson, Elizabeth	1	Colorado	Aug. 16, 1824
		Colorado	Aug. 16, 1824
Tumlinson, James	1	Colorado	Aug. 19, 1824
	½	Wharton	Aug. 19, 1824
	1	Colorado	Aug. 19, 1824
Vandorn, Isaac		(Partner of Daniel E. Baylis)	
Varner, Martin	1	Brazoria	July 8, 1824
		Waller	July 8, 1824
Vince, Allen		(Partner of M. A. Calliham)	
Vince, Richard			
Vince, Robt.	1	Harris	Aug. 21, 1824
Vince, Wm.	1	Harris	July 21, 1824
Walker, James	1	Washington	July 21, 1824
Walker, Thomas		(Partner of Thomas H. Borden)	
Wallice, Caleb	1	Grimes	May 14, 1828
Wells, Francis F.	1	Jackson	July 21, 1824

165

Name		Location	Date
(Wells, Francis F.)	1	Brazoria	July 21, 1824
Westall, Thomas	1	Wharton	July 19, 1824
	1	Fort Bend	July 19, 1824
	2	Austin	July 19, 1824
White, Amy	1	Harris	Aug. 16, 1824
White, Joseph	1	Brazoria	Aug. 16, 1824
White, Reuben	1	Harris	Aug. 19, 1824
White, Walter C.		(Partner of James Knight)	
White, William C.	1	Austin	Aug. 19, 1824
Whitesides, Boland			
Whitesides, Henry	1	Brazos & Grimes	Aug. 10, 1824
Whitesides, James	1	Grimes & Brazos	July 16, 1824
	1	Waller	July 16, 1824
Whitesides, William	1	Waller	July 19, 1824
Whiting, Nath'l		(Partner of Nathan Osborn)	
Whitlock, William	1	Harris	Aug. 16, 1824
Wightman, Elias D.	1	Matagorda	May 25, 1827
Wilkins, Jane	1	Fort Bend	May 26, 1827
Williams, George I.	1	Matagorda	Aug. 19, 1824
Williams, Henry		(Partner of John J. Bowman)	
Williams, John		(Partner of Mills M. Battle)	
Williams, John	1	Waller	Aug. 24, 1824
Williams, John R.	1	(Forfeited)	July 29, 1824
	1	(Forfeited)	July 29, 1824
Williams, Robt. H.	1	Matagorda	Aug. 19, 1824
Williams, Samuel M.	1	Brazoria	Aug. 10, 1824

Name		Location	Date
(Williams, Samuel M.)	1	Brazoria	Aug. 10, 1824
	1	Waller	Aug. 10, 1824
	1	Austin	Aug. 10, 1824
	1	Brazoria	Aug. 10, 1824
Williams, Solomon	1	Matagorda	Aug. 7, 1824
	1	Waller	Aug. 7, 1824
Williams, Thomas	1	Matagorda	Aug. 16, 1824
Woods, Zadock	1	Matagorda	May 15, 1827

Index

169

170

Clark, ———, 79
John C., 14
James, 24
John, 24
Rebecca, 24
Rebekah, 24
Robert, 24
Samuel, 24
Samuel Anthony, 24
Sarah, 24
Thomas, 24
William, 24
Clarke County,
Georgia, 72
Colorado County, 12,
23, 25, 57, 58, 87
Colorado District, 17,
22, 25, 57
Colorado River, 12, 19,
23, 25, 26, 51, 60,
62, 70, 78, 87, 92
Columbia, 45, 63
Columbia County,
Georgia, 47, 48
Columbus, Texas, 12,
22, 57, 58, 87, 91
Comanches, 69
"Come and Take It"
flag, 58
Comstock, Amelia, 89
Rachel Aldrich, 89
William, 89
Constitution of 1824, 9
Consultation of 1835,
19
Convention in 1832, 3,
19
Convention of 1836, 78
Cook, Gustave, 49
Cos, General, 7, 75-76
Cottle, Joseph, 92
Minerva, 92
Cow Creek, 4
Craven County, North
Carolina, 32
Crier, Andrew, 23
Cynthia, 23
James, 25
John, 23
Polly, 23
Rebecca, 25
Tolitha, 23
Crownover, John, 33

Cryer, Barbara, 23
Morgan, 23
Cumberland County,
39
Cumings, Anthony, 24
James, 24
John, 24
Rebecca, 24
Robert, 24
Samuel, 24
Sarah, 24
Thomas, 24
William, 24
Cummins Creek, 22, 25
Cummins, Elinor, 25
Eliza, 25, 58
Harriet, 25
James, 19, 23, 25
Maria, 25
Nancy, 25
Rebecca, 25
Sarah, 25, 65
Willie (or Wylie), 25
Curtis, Frances Carter,
26
James, 79
James, Jr., 27
James, Sr., 26, 27
Polly Ann, 27
Rebecca, 27
Rice III, 26
Sarah Ann, 27
Sarah Hercules, 26,
27, 79
Cushatti (Coshate)
Road, 13

D
Daughters of the
American Revolu-
tion, 39
Daughters of the
Republic of Texas,
82
Davidson County,
Tennessee, 22, 25,
27, 51, 91
Dawson, Captain, 92
DeMoss, Charles, 28
Elizabeth, 28
John, 28
Lewis, 28
Loraharney, 28

Martha (daughter of
Charles), 28
Martha (wife of
Charles), 28
Peter, 28
Sally Lewis, 28
William, 28
Dennet, Mr., 65
Dentley, James, 62
John, 62
Martha, 62
Dewees, W. B., 12, 40
Dinsmore, James, 17
Judith, 17
Dodson, Archeleus B.,
14
Sarah Bradley, 14
Donnell, Martha, 85
Dubois County,
Indiana, 74
Duncan, Molly, 14
Duty, Polly, 23

E
Edgefield District,
South Carolina, 39
Edwards, Jane, 53
Egypt, Texas, 14, 60, 69
Eight Mile Point, 3
Elliott, James, 39
Mary, 39
Este, Edward, 81
Elizabeth, 81
Evergreen, 50

F
Fayette County,
Kentucky, 14
Fayette County, Penn-
sylvania, 67, 69,
70
Fayette County, Texas,
16, 19, 22, 23, 58,
69, 93
Fayetteville, Texas, 23
First Congress of the
Republic of Texas,
20
Fisher, Cynthia, 71
Flag of Independence,
54
Fleming, Mary, 66
Flores, Gaspar, 15

171